CW01302243

paddy toye's DONEGAL

Twelve Walks in The Hills of Donegal

Cottage Publications

First published by Cottage Publications,
An imprint of Laurel Cottage Ltd.
Ballyhay, Donaghadee, N. Ireland 2010.
Copyrights Reserved.
© Paddy Toye 2010.
Maps: Ordnance Survey Ireland Permit No. 8689
© Ordnance Survey Ireland / Government of Ireland
All rights reserved.
No part of this book may be reproduced or stored on any media
without the express written permission of the publishers.
Design & origination in N. Ireland.
Printed & bound in China.
ISBN 978 1 900935 88 3

Front Cover Picture courtesy Mark Devenney

Advice to Walkers

Walkers should be aware that most of the land in Donegal is privately owned and the law in relation to rights-of-way in the Republic of Ireland is fraught with complications and is likely to be the subject of extensive reform in the coming years. In describing the various walks covered in this book we are not claiming that each or any of them is a public right-of-way. The author merely describes the routes that he took – uncontested and without opposition – and we have no view as to their legal status.

The countryside and the people who live and work there should always be treated with respect and following a few simple guidelines will help you and others to enjoy this wonderful county to the fullest extent.

Country Code

- Respect private property, farmland and the rural environment.
- Do not interfere with livestock, crops, machinery or property.
- Guard against all risks of fire, especially near forests.
- Always keep children under close control and supervision.
- Avoid entering farmland containing livestock. Your presence can cause stress to livestock and even endanger your own safety.
- Do not enter farmland if you have dogs with you, even if on a leash, unless with the permission of the landowner.
- Always use gates, stiles, or other recognised access points and avoid damage to fences, hedges and walls.
- Leave all farm gates as you find them.
- Keep the number of cars used to the minimum and park carefully to avoid blocking farm gateways or narrow roads.
- Take all your litter home, leaving only footprints behind.
- Avoid making any unnecessary noise.
- Protect wildlife, plants and trees.
- If following a recognised walking route keep to the waymarked trail.
- If you cause any damage, immediately report it to the farmer or landowner.

ACKNOWLEDGMENTS (IN NO PARTICULAR ORDER)

Neil McCarry
Bridget Sweeny
Paddy Meehan
Stephen Gallagher
Tim Cranley
Michael Gallagher
Laurance McLoone
David Faughnan
Donegal Mountain Rescue
Glenveagh Park
The Bluestack Ramblers

Johnny Gallagher (RIP)
Caitriona Douglas
Seamus Gallagher
Mark Devenney
David Chew
Tom Sweeney
Peter and Annie Magee

And to Paul Kelly, Patricia Daly, Danny Doherty, Marty Crawford and Cheryl Rock for letting me use their internet at all hours of the day and night.
Thanks for all the help and support everyone!

CONTENTS

Introduction 7

Walks

Aghla More, Lough Altan & Aghla Beg 11

The Bluestacks 19

Errigal 27

Muckish 31

Glencolumbkille 39

Glenveagh 45

Gola 57

The Poisoned Glen 61

Slieve League 71

The Sruell Gap 79

The Urris Hills 85

Meenderryherk 89

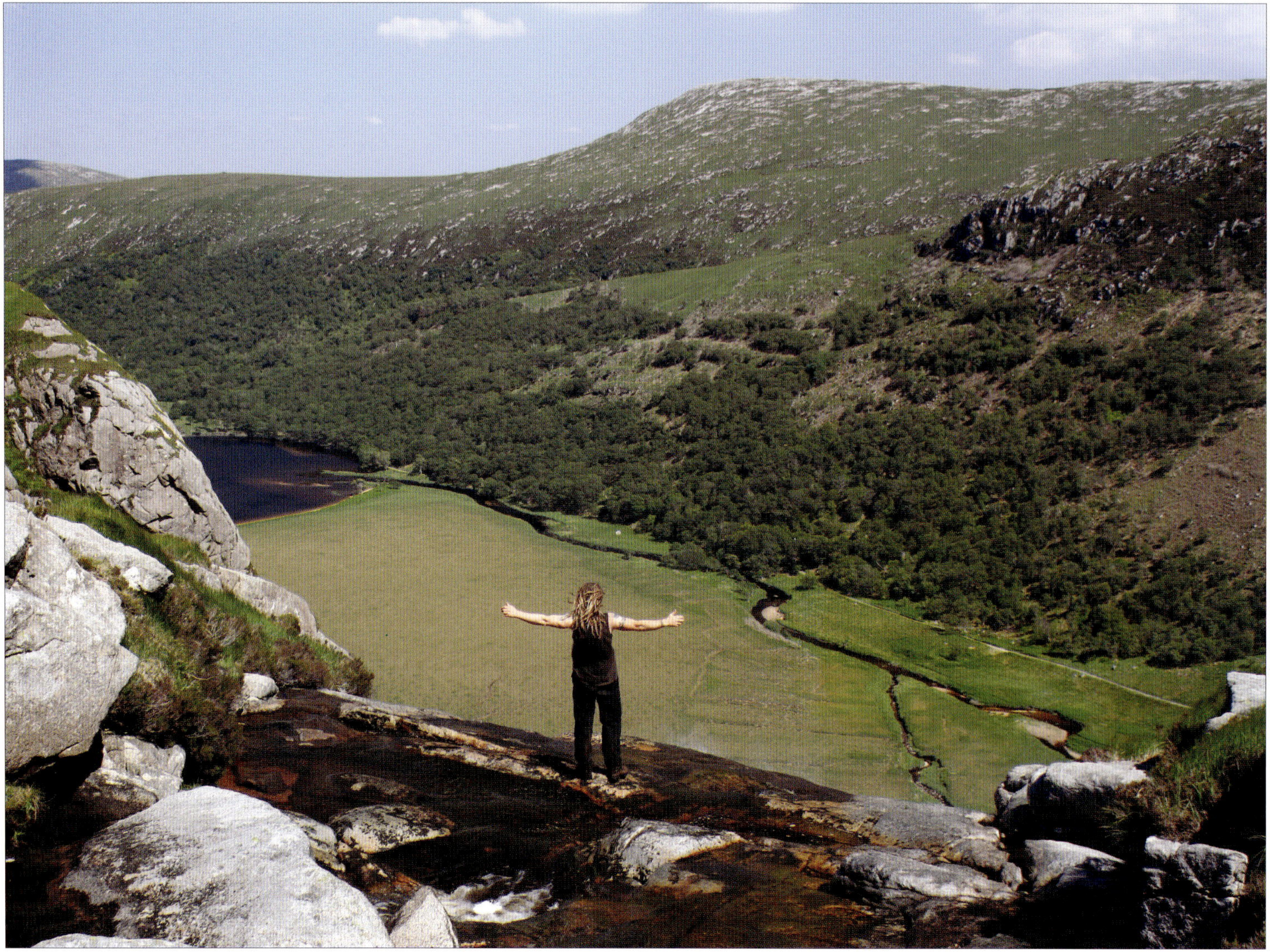

INTRODUCTION

I clearly remember from my early teens the first time the Donegal Highlands cast a spell on me, but unlike so many other things cast aside and forgotten from my youth, the draw of this famous landscape has never left me.

I was travelling with my mother to attend the wake of a distant relative whom I'd probably never met, mesmerised with the inspiring scenery as we bumped along the road between Gleanveigh National Park and Mount Errigal. It was all so very different from the pastoral countryside of my home village of Ballindrait, with its gentle rolling hills and leafy green fields of wide-eyed cattle. While my mother tried to explain the complicated web of family connections that linked us to the wake-house we were visiting, all I could do was gaze out the window in silent awe of the endless panorama of purple, yellow and brown bog that seemed to stretch to infinity. I scarcely imagined the world could be so big. Then, of course, there were the towering hills and mountains that dwarfed everything that dared set eyes on them, reducing us to a level of ant-like insignificance in the presence of such giants. The naked quartzite pyramid of Errigal loomed in the distance like a snapshot from the Himalayas; a stone sentinel, a guardian of time itself, indifferent to the petty quarrels of men and the undisputed keeper of his kingdom in which we were merely humble guests. As I peered at everything in a trance with my face pressed tight against the window, one solitary thought swirled through my mind, a question only a curious delinquent could conjure up: "I wonder what's up there?" I would have to wait a few more years until I found out.

Years later, I left Donegal to do a FÁS course in Outdoor Pursuits on Achill Island, Co. Mayo. I didn't know much about myself back then but I knew I couldn't sit in an office all day and I figured working in an outdoors centre would be a dream job for someone incapable of sitting still for more than ten minutes at a time.

Achill is Ireland's largest island and can easily compete with anywhere on the west coast for dramatic coastal scenery; the ideal location to run a course on outdoor pursuits. Set against this untamed backdrop of sea, mountains and sky, I learned a variety of outdoors skills which included things like map reading, orienteering, night navigation, first aid and countless other little details about walking in the mountains. By the time I'd finished the course I considered myself on a par with Rambo – lacking only the ability to engage entire armies with a couple of shoe laces and a rolled up magazine. It was on these famous mountains and moors of Achill that I learned the skills necessary to make a friend of all wild places, and in writing this book I hope to try and show you how to do the same.

Donegal may well be one of the Third World Counties of the west of Ireland, one of several that's routinely neglected by the string-pullers in Dublin, but there's an upside to this disregard – we have the place to ourselves; or to quote a little verse from Lawrence Donegan's hilarious book, *No News at Throat Lake,* about moving from London to live in Creeslough: *'Donegal, Pride of all, miles and miles of sweet f**k all.'* You might not think this is a huge plus, but if you've visited Kerry or Wicklow in the summer when you're as likely to meet as many family-filled space wagons in a drive through the hills as on Letterkenny Main Street on a busy Saturday then you'll know just how hard it is to find a quiet place to yourself.

Donegal is practically hand-crafted for hill walking and outdoor activities. Of Donegal's 1,193,621 acres, less than half (400,000 acres) is suitable for agriculture, comprising rough pasture, upland bog and mountains. Some 10,117 hectares lie under water in the form of lakes and tidal inlets. It has two major mountain ranges; The Bluestacks in the south and the Derryveaghs in the north, plus a score of smaller ranges and peaks. It has countless lakes and salmon rivers and 120 miles of coastline and blue flag beaches, not to mention peninsulas, islands and fjords similar to Scandinavia. People come from all over the world just for the privilege of setting their eyes on this fabled county. Countless songs have been penned in its name and the people who dwell there are famed for their easy going nature and friendly hospitality. To live in such a place without taking the time to explore it seems absurd to me; like keeping a Picasso in the attic.

The very solitude of the wilderness is its own reward for anyone willing to brave it, or to quote the American author, Edward Abbey: *'Wilderness is not a luxury but a necessity of the human spirit.'*

In this book I will attempt to lead you on some of the walks that have inspired me; places of bleak, yet profound beauty and jaw dropping scenery that no camera, however expensive, can faithfully reproduce. Some of the walks in this book are quite long, requiring a reasonable level of fitness and a little preparation before you can attempt them. Others, however, won't require you as special guest appearance on the popular TV series *999 Lifesavers*. Some of the walks are well known, while others are simply ones I made up myself. Let me take you off the beaten track and in doing so, perhaps inspire you to go out there and find your own little piece of Donegal; and remember this should you ponder it: Nothing of any worth was ever achieved sitting on the sofa in front of the TV (apart from putting your foot through it).

Paddy Toye
paddytoye@hotmail.com

Safety

The lack of paths and trails in the mountains of Donegal means that traversing them requires a little more planning than your average walk in the park. The Donegal Mountain Rescue averages around 25 – 30 call-outs a year. They range in nature from people becoming lost in poor visibility, which can lead to exposure and hypothermia; lower leg injuries resulting from twists, slips and rock climbers falling and sustaining multiple fractures. In 2008 the DMR dealt with 2 fatalities, 3 lower leg injuries, 1 back injury and 2 cases of exhaustion and a case of hypothermia. The other stats comprised despondent individuals, including a group of 6 teenagers who were benighted on Slieve League and several hill-based and charity events which resulted in people losing their way due to bad weather and poor navigational skills. Muckish Mountain, Errigal and Slieve League are particular hotspots when it comes to these types of call-outs. Inappropriate clothing and a casual attitude can easily result in hypothermia if the weather suddenly changes and you become lost, cold and disoriented. Thankfully, there are a few simple things you can do to prevent such an unfavourable outcome: Don't go alone until you have some experience. Don't go in bad weather and if the weather changes and closes in when you're out, turn back. Always tell someone where you're going and your estimated time for arriving home. Bring a phone but don't depend on it as mountains aren't conducive to phone signals. Bring an OSI Discovery Series map and familiarise yourself with the route you intend to take (the maps in this book are for illustration only). A compass is fine but only if you know how to use it. Wear appropriate clothing for hill walking and have waterproofs in a rucksack and some extra clothes in case you get wet. No matter how brightly the sun is shining, pack your rucksack as if you're expecting a monsoon. Never wear denim. Denim takes ages to dry and once it's wet, it'll chill your legs. Man-made polyesters are best as your body still retains heat even when they're wet and they dry quickly in the breeze. As well as your lunch bring a little extra food in case there's an emergency and you have to wait to be rescued. And above all – don't panic if you get lost. Like most things in life a little common sense goes a long way and hill walking is no different.

Summary

- Study the route beforehand.
- Get the weather forecast.
- Dress sensibly. Wear boots. Take waterproofs and extra warm clothing.
- Take ample food and drink for the journey.
- Carry map, compass and whistle.
- Avoid travelling alone on unfamiliar walks.
- Leave details of your route with someone and give them your expected time of return.
- Report your return.
- Keep to paths and take heed of warning signs, they are there for your protection, and take special care on country roads.

Ascending Aghla More

Aghla More, Lough Altan & Aghla Beg

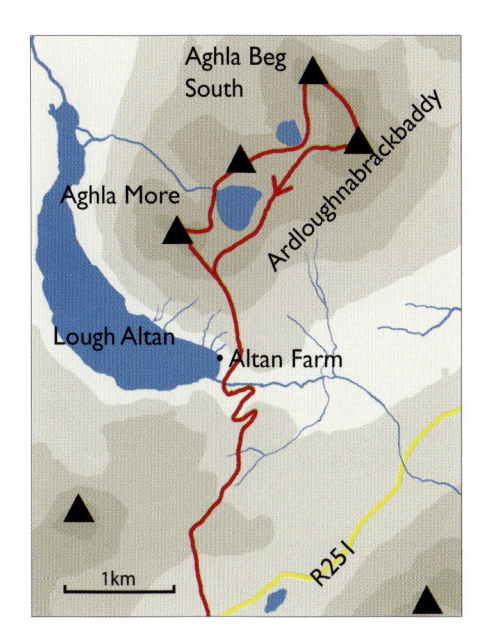

OS Map: 1 and 2
Time: 5 to 6 hours

This walk was included in a recent *Irish Times* 'Book of Irish Walks' supplement, and frankly, if it's good enough for the *Irish Times* then it's good enough for me. It begins with a leisurely dander over the bog to Lough Altan immediately followed by a lung-busting assault to the top of Aghla More (584m) and a meander around its siblings Aghla Beg (564m) and Aghla Beg South (603m), which is also known as Ardloughnabrackbaddy for reasons we'll probably never truly understand. Perhaps Aghla Beg South was just too easy to pronounce?

The walk begins on a barely visible path over the bog which begins on the main road between Glenveagh and Gweedore (R251). The path is marked on the OS map, near little Lough Sand on the opposite side of the road. It's quite close to Mount Errigal (751m) and the first twenty feet of the path is covered in loose stones which makes it stand out in the endless bog. Beyond that it's a just a faint outline in the hills. The path was once the gateway to the old ruined building, a castle-like structure known as Altan Farm, which stands lonesome and windswept on the howling shores of Lough Altan and is undoubtedly one of the highlights of this walk.

Following the path, it takes roughly an hour to reach the castle. (Even though it's commonly known as Altan Farm, I simply cannot bring myself to refer to it as a farm when it so clearly resembles a castle – not that it was a castle or anything, but it improves the narrative flow of words to refer to it as a castle – so there). Its position on a bank overlooking the lough, which glistens like an enormous water-filled

Altan Farm with Aghla More in background

pothole of shimmering blue, squeezed between the imposing twin towers of Aghla More and Mackoght (555m), is nothing short of spectacular with a long strand of fine white sand running the length of the lough like a blue flag beach. The stream that empties into it next to the castle boasts several stunning waterfalls and you can even spy the sea in the far-off distance.

I've written articles about this mysterious building for the local press in an attempt to unlock some information about its history and origins, but without much success. Even the supplement in the *Irish Times* could shed no light on the subject but I was damned if it was going to beat me.

Finally I put an advert in the *Donegal Democrat* requesting information and, several weeks later, was contacted by an elderly woman who not only knew the story, but was directly connected to it by way of her grandfather.

She told me that in 1860 a Dublin solicitor called Mr. Oban Woodhouse came across Lough Altan and decided he'd procure it for himself as a site for his new summer residence. At the time the area, which included 1500 acres of the surrounding bog, was farmed by a man named Hughie Sweeney, also known as Hughie Altan to distinguish him from his uncles who were also called Hughie. Originally there were two cottages on the site; Hughie and his young family had one and a woman called Nancy Logue, from Crosskill, who spun and wove for a living, the other. Mr. Oban swiftly evicted everyone and Hughie was given £75 and a house at the back of Muckish Mountain by way of compensation.

Needless to say, Hughie was none too impressed with the arrangement and the Red Coats had to be drafted in to ensure Hughie didn't attempt to take repossession of his home before the two cottages were demolished and their stone used to build the walls around the castle.

Some years later, the local landlord of the area, a man by the surname of Stewart, asked Hughie do to a job for him which Hughie refused. For his act of defiance the landlord evicted Hughie from his second home behind Muckish Mountain, whereupon once again Hughie gathered up his family and made his way across the mountains to a place called Pruckless in the locality of Cloughaneely, where he settled and raised his family. He was the first Sweeney in Pruckless and his home can still be seen standing today as a little barn behind what became the home of his grand-daughter, Bridget Sweeney, who carefully recounted the tale to me at the ripe old age of 93.

But the story didn't end there… While employing local men to build the road (the path from the main road) out to his new castle-like summer residence, poor Mr. Woodhouse ran out of funds to complete it and ended up having to sell his new summer house to a Scottish shepherd for the sum of £50. After that it passed into the hands of the Bishop of Raphoe, who purchased it with the intention of turning it into a school for priests (which never materialised), after which it passed through the hands of several other owners and now stands as an empty shell of forgotten memories.

The whole area has a certain feel about it which escapes me every time I try and put it into words. The presence of the old ruin, its ever watchful gaze over the vast blue expanse of cobalt blue, and the almost vertical slopes of rock that descend from the

Altan Farm and Lough Altan

Waterfall at the start of the climb

heavens, slicing through the water without regard for the petty endeavours of man, all add to a feeling of inexplicable tranquil isolation that I've not experienced anywhere else. There's something about the water too; constantly in the shadow of mountains, its hue never alters from the deepest shades of blue, as if the bottom is beyond even the reach of the fish that swim in it. Yet it all feels oddly familiar too, welcoming somehow. Maybe it's just me. I'd like to know what Hughie Altan thought about the place before his untimely departure. These, however, are merely words and words are no substitute for experience. Go and see for yourself.

Party time over, now the hard part of the walk begins in earnest. Follow the stream back a little way to the last waterfall and then steer yourself up the slopes towards the top of Aghla More and prepare for a monumental slog that makes the assault course on Gladiators seem like a relaxing spa break in Paris. Now's the time to scribble down your last will and testament and make those hasty last minute phone calls (if you can get reception) to friends and loved ones. Yes, there are bigger mountains, but the ascent from the shores of Altan really is an immense pain in the backside – and legs – but nothing ventured, nothing gained. Actually, it's not too bad in the beginning but about halfway up you'll begin to ask yourself some very searching questions regarding your sanity, i.e., why the hell did I start this? As fit as I am, by halfway, I too, was seriously considering collapsing in a heap and rolling helplessly back down the mountain like a rolled up corpse in a carpet, but experience dictated that the sense of achievement at reaching the top would far outweigh the sense of disappointment of landing the bottom – not to mention a potentially fractured skull. It's on mountains like these you really do ask yourself why? What is it about hill walkers that draws them from the comfort of their armchairs into the back of beyond. Escapism? Possibly. Maybe some people are just made for walking. Maybe it's a craving for those big skies and wide horizons, for a certain kind of light alien to towns and cities. Maybe, for some, the modern world just moves too fast and the only way they can slow it down to a pace which suits them is to get away from it all, if only for a while. In a technological society that strives, rightly or wrongly, to reduce even the simplest of everyday tasks to the push of a button, negating the need for thought and action, some people just need to cut loose and revert back to a slightly earlier stage in man's development, when self sufficiency, wits, courage, endurance and common sense reigned supreme. There's definitely a therapeutic quality involved in this madness, a feeling of independence, a strength of will to complete something you set out to finish, no matter how loudly your legs are screaming. When you begin any big walk in the mountains there's always a moment of uncertainty, a lingering reservation that makes a hasty retreat for home seem like a very appealing option. But keep going until you've gone too far to turn back – past the point of no return – and you'll cross that invisible barrier in your mind, banishing the wavering clouds of doubt that shadow us every time we face the unknown. Passing the point of no return is almost always followed by a mild feeling of triumph, joyful independence and freedom. You could say it's a little of all these things that makes people take to the hills, and it is, but for me the deciding factor is nothing more than simple curiosity. When I gaze up at a mountain I want to know what the world looks like from up there, looking down, instead of down here looking up. Perhaps there's something up there that I should know about? Or I wonder what's on the other side. I don't want to gaze and wonder – I want to know. Ignoring the mountains is like living next to a wonderful little bar and never being bothered enough to venture in and sample a pint, scope out the vibe and harass the barmaids. Maybe I've just got too much

Looking back from the slopes of Aghla More

damn time on my hands? Maybe so, but anyone with even planning permission for a brain will agree that an increased knowledge of your environment can only colour and enrich your life. When you finally do make it home from a hard day's tramp about the rocks and heather, you'll spend the rest of the day wallowing deservedly in a haze of blissful exhaustion; a hue in your cheeks, a glint in your eye and the song of the wind in your hair – if you have any.

Now where was I? Oh yes – halfway up Aghla More on the verge of a stroke. When you do finally reach the top you'll be delighted to discover the summit is very central and not spread out into an infuriating scattering of other little will-crushing peaks. You'll also probably be a little shocked to find that you've suddenly come to the edge of a cliff, as the other side has an almost sheer face as it plunges towards Lough Altan below. On reaching the top, one is overcome with a feeling of elation (relief) that I've rarely felt on any other mountain, and when you see the view over the cliff's edge for the first time you may have to affix sellotape across your eyes to prevent them from popping out of their sockets. There can be no doubt that the summit of Aghla More is the very best place in the county to view the county's tallest mountain, Errigal, with the majestic Derryveaghs playing a fantastic supporting role in the background. Most people only ever see Errigal from the passing window of a car or from postcards and photographs, and from these pedestrian vistas it always looks the same, an imposing solid triangle of rock. But the view from Aghla is completely new and different to the one we're accustomed to, and it reveals a side of the quartz giant we rarely see. From Aghla, mighty Errigal doesn't look so mighty anymore, and appears to lurch forward as if it was slowly beginning to melt like an enormous slab of ice cream. It requires only a deft tinkering of the imagination to picture the glaciers, which formed and shaped the mountain, sliding down to the right and carving out the characteristic shapes in the landscape which are now so familiar to us. This one snapshot of Errigal is more informative than ten geography lessons with endless descriptions and diagrams. You'll become completely absorbed happily studying the fascinating shapes and forms of the view before you. Looking west towards Cashelnagor you can make out the little patchwork of green fields salvaged from the bog wherever there's human habitation and be-

From the top of Aghla looking towards Errigal, Mackoght and the Derryveaghs

yond that you can clearly see Arran More and all the way up to Bloody Foreland. Although you're looking directly across at Errigal, which is taller, it actually feels like you're looking down on it. Plus, unlike Errigal, you probably won't have to share Aghla with bus loads of day trippers who regularly make the pilgrimage up Errigal during the summer months.

Leaving Aghla, head down the slopes, keeping to the right to avoid the steep descent, and head for the left hand side of Lough Feeane and make your way to the top of the furthest peak of Aghla Beg, going across the slope rather than straight up to take advantage of the gentler rise, and then head back across the saddle to the higher peak of Aghla Beg South, (Ardloughnabrackbaddy).

Although Aghla Beg North is smaller than Aghla Beg South, it's clearly more popular if cairn size is anything to go by. The one on Aghla Beg North looks like it was deposited there by a dump truck compared to the one on Aghla Beg South, which resembles a tiny rockery in the corner of some garden, assembled by a drunk who passed out before he could complete it.

From these peaks there's commanding views of Muckish and Lough Aluirg as well as a good stretch of coastline including views of Tory, Inishbofin and Horn Head. As you turn for home in the same general direction you came from, it may occur to you that, wandering around the rocky slopes, all you can see is mountains, deep blue lakes, the endless sky and the sea in the distance. At such points you may just snatch a fleeting sense of what it might feel like to be the last person on earth – which nowadays one doesn't feel too often, if ever.

Aghla Beg North and South over Lough Feeane

The Bluestack Mountains, clouds and cairns

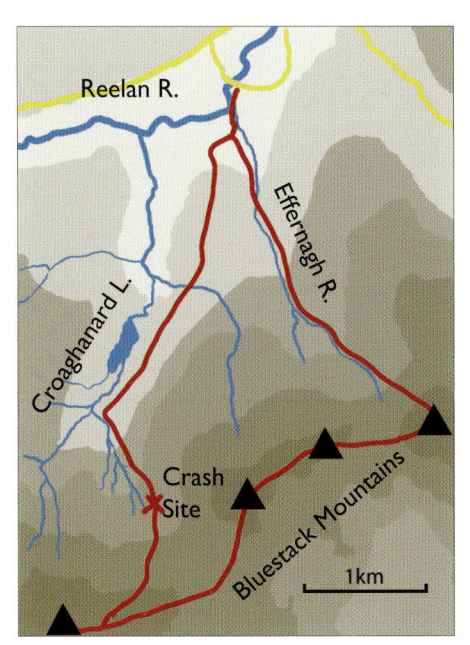

MAP: SHEET 11
TIME: 5 TO 6 HOURS

THE BLUESTACKS

This walk was my first ever excursion into the peaks of the famous Bluestack Mountains. Like a letter I'd been meaning to write, getting acquainted with these hills seemed, for me, to be forever on the long finger. I'd driven around them a few times, circling them like a wolf stalking its prey, stopping and squinting and suddenly disappearing down some little road to see where it went. Lots of little roads, lots of things to see, lots of places for a man to get lost – wonderful. A discussion about the Bluestacks will invariably result in someone coining the well-worn phrase about them having their own independent weather system. I'd like to personally vouch for this as on my first ever trip I found myself stranded on one of the many peaks, engulfed in a thick soup of clouds when only moments before I was deciding what factor sun cream to use. I had to sit it out until the weather cleared, which thankfully it did.

The walk itself follows a wild and wonderful stream into the heart of the hills, followed by a saunter up to the highest peak in the Bluestacks (674m) and then down, via the valley of the crash site of Sunderland DW-110, before ending up like it started, following a rocky stream down off the hills and back to the beginning.

On the main road from Ballybofey to Dungloe (R252) turn off at the junction for Welchtown at a chapel on a bend in the road, signposted for Glenties and *An Coimín*. (R253). Head down this road until you pass Commeen and keep going until you see a turn off on the left, signposted for *Na Cruacha*. Pretty soon you'll come to a little roadside grotto at another junction on the left with a

Bridge on Effernagh River

ramblers' signpost which reads *Bealach na Taeltachta slí na Finne*. Take this left and drive until you can go no further, crossing the Reelan River on a wee, flat, wall-less bridge at the bottom of the hill and stopping to get out to open (and close) a gate in order to get past.

Without even getting out of the car you're already deep in Bluestack Country, at the foot of the great hills that make this area such an outstanding spectacle of nature. When you cross the little bridge take the dirt path on the right, park where it meets the Effernagh River and follow the flow upstream right into Glascarns Hill. There is a path through the forestry on the other side of the Effernagh River, but an impenetrable wall of boring lifeless trees can't compete with hopping about waterfalls and skipping over boulders like a buck goat all the way to the summit.

The Effernagh is arguably the most beautiful mountain

Effernagh River

stream I've ever had the pleasure to wander through; a vein of exposed rock reaching down the hillside, sculpted by countless years of endless toil by the water that rises from deep within the hills. It's also a relatively easy stroll to the hilltops as the walk along the river maintains a gentle and measured gradient for most of the way. As the river dissolves into a trickle and finally submits to the earth, you should come across a single enormous tractor-sized boulder sitting alone, easily distinguishable from the litany of other more modest-sized rocks. From roughly around here, make a beeline for tiny Lough Aduff nestled in the peaks and as you reach the top you should see in the distance a scattering of big flat rocks which are ideally placed for walking on as you break for the horizon.

As soon as you reach the top of these rocks – bang – you're in the middle of the mountains looking out towards Lough Eske and beyond, with fantastic views of the Bluestack's barren and beautiful landscape. From up here walking along the high points is a breeze and a joy as you look across at Donegal's other famous mountain range, the Derryveaghs, seeing them all in one long string of peaks, and out towards Barnesmore Gap and all the way down to the hills and mountains of Sligo and Leitrim.

Make your way west along the peaks until something rather odd in the distance catches your eye. You won't have to make a huge effort to spot it

On top, Lough Eske in background

because its colour in the mountains is so out of place it makes it clearly visible from miles away. At first I thought I was seeing things; my eyes tried to convince me I was looking at a huge stack of bagged turf in white fertiliser bags, which from a mile away is exactly what it looks like, but my brain refused to accept it, arguing relentlessly that farmers generally don't find, stack and bag turf 1800 feet above sea level. But what the heck else

Marble outcrop

could it be, this huge white mound in the distance, like there was a sudden fall of snow in one tiny isolated spot? I've seen some strange things in the mountains but never in my life did I come across an outcrop of almost pure sparking white marble like the one up in the Bluestacks. The mind boggles as you approach it and finally accept what it is. Even on the overcast day that it was I could feel my eyes contract and retreat at the reflected glare from this fantastic geological oddity – this sparkling white jewel of nature's creation bursting through the rock on the edge of the cliff overlooking the valley below. I'd wager you'd need dark glasses to look at it on a sunny day. It's even visible from way down below at the roadside if you know where to look.

From this marble signpost make your way around the edge of the mountains, like walking along the rim of a giant bowl, and head towards the highest point of the Bluestacks. There's a scattering of cairns along the edge of the mountain as you face south west on your approach to the tallest peak. As you near the top you'll come to a sheep fence which has a stile especially built for walkers to use, in order to cross over without damaging the fence.

Once the fence is crossed the summit is only a few minutes away. From this eagle-eyed vantage point you can probably see more of the county than at any other place I know of; the Derryveaghs, Errigal, Inishowen, Donegal Bay, the cliffs and headlands around Slieve League, the Sperrin Mountains in Tyrone and the mountains of Sligo and Leitrim (and the Bluestacks in which you're standing, obviously). Not too shabby, I think you'll agree.

To get down, head back to where you crossed the sheep fence, hop back over the stile, and follow the fence down off the mountain. Keep going until you can see Lough Croaghanard and a meandering stream snaking its way towards it in the distance.

However, rather than going straight down, it's worth stopping and casting your mind back half a century to a dark, foul night near the end of the Second World War.

Though not publicly known at the time, during WWII there was an agreement between Ireland and Britain which allowed the RAF to fly over a forty mile corridor above the River Erne to facilitate getting flying boats from the British Air Force base at Castle Archdale to the Atlantic where they searched for German U-boats.

On the night of 31st January 1944 a Sunderland Mark III Flying Boat, DW-110, with a crew of twelve, set out from Wales to relieve another crew from the same squadron which was already out on patrol. On the completion of their mission DW-110 was instructed to divert to Castle Archdale in Fermanagh on account of bad weather in Wales. By many accounts it was a terrible night as the rain swept down through a fog of clouds that hugged the mountains in a shroud of darkness.

The plane was both seen and heard by the locals around Glenties and the surrounding areas as it headed towards the mountains, miles off the official corridor route around the Donegal Bay area. Way off-course, in bad visibility and scrambling for a radio fix through the impenetrable barrier of granite, the crew had no way of knowing the collision course they were on with the mountains that lay ahead.

The following are extracts from an interview with the last known survivor of the crash, rear-gunner Jim Gilchrist, which was broadcast on Highland Radio a few years ago.

Donegal Bay hidden by changeable weather

A piece of the wreckage of Dw-110

"…I woke up on the ground with rain on my face and banging and crashing and explosions going on. I was only 25 metres away from the aircraft at the time… I have no idea how I got there… the most abiding memory that I have is the fin of the aircraft and the tail plane of the aircraft, like some huge burning cross – it was a most extraordinary experience.

"We had no idea where we were, we sheltered as far as we could for the rest of the night. We knew we were in Ireland, but we had no idea precisely where we were. And when dawn came, as far as we could see we were in a mountainous area… no sign of roads or buildings or people – just nothing but mountains and more mountains. We set off and after – it must have been about six hours of climbing down the mountain – we eventually began to see that there was a little cottage about perhaps a half, or three quarters, of a mile in front of us. We had to wade across a stream and when we got to the other side we suddenly saw that there was a lady there with children all around her, clutching her skirts – she looked somewhat nervous, frightened – it's not surprising, as she could not have ever seen the people who were coming towards her, dressed the way we were and matted in blood."

"Her name was Catherine McDermott and she turned out to be – for me at least – the gentlest woman I've ever come across in my life. She was a saint of a woman – although she was fearful – she recognised immediately that we were in need of help and assistance and what little she had, which was not much, she shared with us. She was a widow and her children were

Memorial to the crash victims

around her… It was an incredible situation. She was an incredible woman. I've never forgotten her… I spoke later to her

24

son Joe; they heard an explosion during the night and they must have had some idea that we were connected with that event… She [Catherine] *didn't have much English, she was mainly a Gaelic speaking lady. Her son Joe went off with Gowens (who had not been as badly injured as me) to a local Garda station and sometime later a rescue party arrived; priests, soldiers and so on and so forth… the rescue and the recovery of the dead began."*

The final resting place of DW-110 is over to the right, near the top, in an area of hillside where the rocks are more prominent. Looking up on the ridge you should be able to clearly see the white outcrop of quartz jutting out of the mountain. Finding the crash site requires a little searching around but I found it without too much trouble. On the OS map it's approximately on top of the A in the word STACKS where BLUE STACK MOUNTAINS is printed across the mountains. Fragments of wreckage guide you to some big rocks where a plaque, unveiled in 1988 by Jim Gilchrist, commemorates the victims of the crash.

From this area on the hillside you'll be able to clearly see Lough Croaghanard and to return to the starting point it's simply a matter of following one of the streams which run down the hill and into the Lough; the same route taken by the survivors of the plane crash all those years ago. As you near the Lough keep to the high ground on the right so as to avoid the heavily forested area around the Lough which is extremely difficult to walk through. Keep going until you either hit a path, or the Reelan River, either of which will bring you back to where you started.

The path home

Errigal, Donegal's highest peak

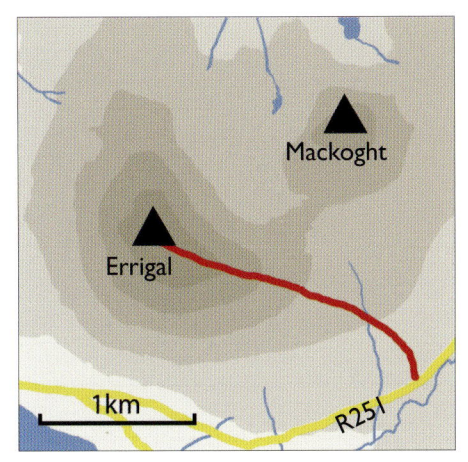

OS Map: 1
Time: 2–3 hours

errigal

This is one of the shortest chapters in the book, and one of the easiest walks, but it would be foolish to write a book about hill walking in Donegal and leave out Errigal. Even the very word 'Errigal' sounds inspiring when rolled off the tongue. The County's highest peak, Errigal truly is a giant among giants. Standing at an impressive 751 metres, on a clear day its unmistakable steeple is visible from almost any moderately-sized hilltop in the County. It's kind of like Donegal's unofficial 'Bat Signal.'

Because of its size, Errigal always manages to sneak into and gatecrash pictures of other mountains, whether you want it in the shot or not. It's just always there. What are you supposed to do? You can't very well ask it to move.

Despite Errigal's heavyweight title, it's surprisingly easy to climb, which a lot of people simply don't realise. "Errigal," they say, "are you mad?" Or else it's: "Oh aye, Errigal, I've always been meaning to, but…" If you're reading this and you've never scaled the quartz giant, you now have no further excuses.

Located near Dunlewy on the main Dunlewy to Gweedore road (R251), Errigal is ideally located for observing the Highlands of Donegal. Situated at the beginning of a smaller chain of mountains known as The Seven Sisters, Errigal fits snugly between her six sisters and the Derryveaghs to the south across the Valley. As well as the Derryveaghs, there's eagle-eyed views of The Poisoned Glen, Dunlewy, Dunlewy Lough and Lough Nacung Upper. The Seven Sisters include Errigal, Mackoght (little Errigal), Aghla More, Aghla Beg, Ardloughnabrackbaddy, Crocknalaragagh and Muckish.

At the foot of Errigal, at the main

Errigal, Mackoght and Beaghy

road, there's a little walled car park for hikers. It usually has at least a couple of cars, or a bus parked up, which is testament to the popularity of the mountain. The well-worn path up Errigal follows a ridge up the east-facing slope and its mark on the mountainside is visible from miles away. If you stop your car and pull over, you can usually make out people like tiny ants making their way along the path. I've often met bus loads of elderly folk, sticks in hand, braving the slopes so there really is no excuse for never having been up there.

In the early stages, the path crosses bog and heath and the gradient is easy on the legs, but the further you go the steeper it gets and in the latter stages the path becomes a steep scree slope

Hare Tracks on Errigal

where a person could easily twist an ankle, or two. Still, anyone of average fitness could reach the summit in just over an hour. The last time I climbed Errigal was on Christmas Eve 2009/10 in three feet of snow and, on that particular trip, I ran into a man and his two sons trudging their way to the top in jeans, wellies and t-shirts! They were obviously professionals.

Near the top, the path levels off onto a narrow shoulder where you'll encounter a small windbreak where previous walkers have put the abundance of rocks to good use to build a tiny shelter. You might want to take a break here out of the wind before the final saunter to the peaks.

If you've never scaled Errigal you might be surprised to discover that Errigal actually has two separate peaks, separated by a narrow ridge; which, on a windy day, can be quite a hair-raising experience – literally. It's like a mini version of the One Man's Pass on Slieve League. From below, Errigal often looks like a perfect pyramid, but when you're on top you can clearly see the twin peaks. It's as though some giant took a mouthful out of the top of the mountain, leaving a perfect bite mark which makes up the little valley between the two peaks. The word Errigal itself means 'oratory' but there's little or no evidence of any ancient religious settlements similar to that on the slopes of Slieve League.

Errigal's other peak

It's probably more likely a reference to the spire-like shape of the mountain; visible for miles, it may have reminded Ireland's first Christians of the Church spires and monasteries of Europe.

Muckish Mountain

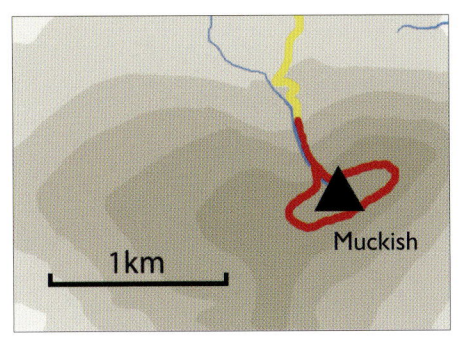

OS Map: 2
Time: 2 to 3 hours

muckish

Muckish Mountain, The Pig's Back, The Table Top, The Ironing Board, The Big M (ok, I made those last few up), call it what you will, there's no mistaking Muckish. Rising from the earth like the barnacle-encrusted hull of some gigantic ship run aground, its commanding presence dominates the landscape for miles around and all the way out to sea. Only its big brother, Errigal, can compete with Muckish for sheer character and distinctive individuality. Muckish, like Errigal, is as Donegal as they come, an instantly recognisable symbol of the county – like The Sean Doherty Show, milk cartons with cows on them, Oatfield Sweets, Football Special or self-replicating potholes that magically reappear the day after they've been filled in.

Just like there's more than one way to skin a cat, there's more than one way to scale a mountain, but for me you can't beat the Miners' Path on the north-facing slope. I've climbed Muckish several times before but only recently discovered the Miners' Path which zig-zags its way up an almost sheer slope to a disused quarry at the top. To reach the starting point drive through Creeslough town and turn left off the main road (N56) down a wee back road signposted for Derryharriff. The turnoff is easy to find as it's directly opposite a graveyard on the other side of the road. Continue down this road until you pass a quarry on the right shortly followed by a junction. Go left at the junction, passing over a cattle grid, and this will take you up to the starting point into the heart of the mountain. As you pass over the cattle grid, glance to your left and you'll clearly see the embankments of the old railway line that ran from Falcarragh to Derry. At this point watch out for the sheep, whose endearing habits include playing chicken with any oncoming traffic and communal sunbathing on

Approach lane to the quarry and Miners' Path

had to slog up and down it.

In the early stages, parts of the path are quite steep and covered in rubble. I'd advise more mature walkers to bring a stick for balance, as the going underfoot can be a tad slippy with all the loose rocks. After the steep climb over the rubble, you'll reach a small wooden staircase that brings you up to where the path begins a long and increasingly dramatic zig-zag to the top. The little wooden staircase merits a mention by the mere fact of its existence; you just don't expect to find a wooden staircase perched up a mountain – it's just great. (If it's not already apparent, I'm very easily amused – extremely hard to impress though).

As you progress upwards in a diagonal march across the mountainside it's easy to lose track of the path as the ground is badly broken up, eroded, and buried under little landslides in places. Every now and then it's advisable to stop and have a look around to see where you're going. You might even have to make the odd little detour to relocate the path should you

blind corners slap-bang in the middle of the road.

At the foot of the mountain you'll come to two big concrete blocks, one of which (on the right) has the word START, and a directional arrow painted on it in faded red letters. This is the beginning of the Miners' Path.

After about ten minutes you should come to the first of six or seven stone staircases which punctuate the climb to the summit. Discovering staircases on a mountain, with steps cut into the solid rock, is guaranteed to arouse a childish grin of awe and wonder which adds a certain novelty to the proceedings, although the same probably can't be said for the miners who

A mountain staircase

An old wooden staircase in the Quarrys

lose it. Be sure to stay vigilant because at one point, halfway up, the path appears to go right around the edge of the sheer cliff face, but let me assure you firsthand that this is not a very productive route to follow, especially if you've become accustomed to breathing and are relatively content with the general layout of your limbs and internal organs. The ravens have enough to eat without laying out a banquet for them. Near the top the stone steps hug the rock as they spiral upwards like a staircase in some medieval castle, set against a stunning backdrop of mountain, moors and the sea, with Tory Island in the distance.

Evidence of the mountain's industrious past lie scattered throughout the jagged slopes in the form of antique ma-

Quarry at top of Muckish

chinery, winches and engines, which once ferried cargoes of sand up and down the slopes. It must have been quite the scene when the quarry was fully operational, the entire cliff echoing with the sound of men and mechanical toil. The old winches and pulleys have long since retired, their wheels and cogs silently rusting among the rocks and boulders. The only sound the mountain hears now is the toneless croak of ravens nesting on the cliffs – and the wind. One man I was lucky enough to meet with didn't have to imagine what the quarry was like because he worked there in his youth; Johnny Gallagher from Creeslough:

"I started work there when I was 16, that was in 1946. You had to start work at eight in the morning and your pay didn't start until you reached the top of the mountain. Then there was days you'd have got nothing if it rained and you couldn't work. You'd be stuck in the wee hut all day waiting for the rain to stop. It might have been raining on the top and grand down below, or the other way round. Nobody had any waterproofs or protective clothes in those days. Manys the time I had to carry up a five gallon gerrycan of diesel to the generator at the top. You'd take a can up with you when you were going up in the morning. There were wee buggies at the top and we'd fill them with sand by shovel and then they'd go down the chute, and it would get washed at another stop halfway down the mountain. They took the sand down to the pier at Ards and it went away on the boats to England and Germany. The sand was of a very fine grade, pure white, and was used in glass making. I think Waterford Crystal might have used it too. It was so fine it got into everything; it would be in your clothes and you'd be chewing it in your sandwiches at teatime."

Abandoned machinery in the quarry

When I last went up there for the purposes of writing this book, all I took with me was my camera and a notebook – I sure as hell was glad I didn't have a five gallon can of diesel on my back, and you will be too, believe me. When you finally reach the quarry at the top, the first thing you realise is that it's not actually the top and you've a little way to go before you can break out the flag and pose for photographs. The quarry is an enormous gash in the rock face with veins of white and red sand clearly visible against the darker coloured rock like the layers in a cake. Several hunks of banjaxed machinery lie rusting at the quarry's edge overlooking the entire scene like a heavily shelled defensive position of a

The view north towards Tory Island and Inisbofin

battlement from some forgotten war.

The top of Muckish itself is like the world's biggest putting green covered in jagged white blocks of quartz; the ideal location for testing a moon buggy but not so good for golf. In the middle of the mountain there's a huge cairn, probably containing the remains of some ancient warrior chieftain. From the top there are fantastic views of the Derryveaghs and all along the coastline from Gortahork to Downings.

The huge steel cross on top of Muckish weighs half a ton and getting it up there almost caused an international incident with our neighbours across the border. Originally there was a wooden cross where the new one stands, erected in 1950 by the miners. Supervised by John Brogan, the old cross was taken up in pieces and assembled at the top. Over time it rotted and fell apart so in 2000 it was decided to replace it with a more durable, permanent, one and every house of worship that fell under the gaze of Muckish had a collection for the completion of the project. When the Irish army was asked for assistance in getting the cross to its final destination they politely declined, saying it was too heavy for their helicopters. The British army stationed in Ballykelly was then asked to help, which they agreed to, but first they needed permission from the Irish army to cross the border. Low and behold, in an act of divine intervention, two Irish army helicopters were suddenly dispatched from Finnar Army camp to save the day, and their blushes, and finally the new cross stood in place on the mountain. On the day of its blessing, in a touching act of community spirit, hundreds from congregations of every religion came together as one atop the windswept summit for the blessing ceremony of the new cross. It's a pity we couldn't all get along like that all the time. This really is an enjoyable and rewarding walk steeped in history and local lore. And if all that isn't enough, a look at the Ordnance Survey map will show the mountain's highest point is 666 metres.

No wonder there's a cross up there.

The cross at the top of Muckish

The huge cairn on top of Muckish

View of Glencolumbkille and Glen Bay

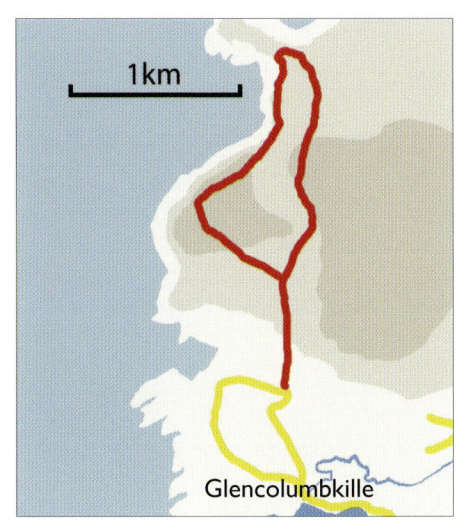

OS Map: 10
Time: 3 to 4 hours

Glencolumbkille

This beautiful glen, tucked safely away in south-west Donegal, is often described as one of the county's best kept secrets. On a good day the glen, which bears the name of the great St. Colmcille, is like a wilderness paradise of land, cliffs, sea and sky. A place for wandering aimlessly around, in no real hurry to be anywhere in particular. St. Comcille came to the glen to meditate, preach and pray. Commemorated with 12 crosses, the path he walked while meditating is still used by the people today and is part of this walk.

A quick glance at the OS map will show that the whole area is awash with signs of life from Ireland's ancient past. The little village has one of the healthiest collections of cairns, megalithic tombs and standing stones that I've ever seen gathered together in one area. Many of the ancient stone crosses were probably pagan in origin and later Christianised in Colmcille's time by adding lines and circles to the original pagan designs. Steeped in all this history, with actual physical evidence of a time when Ireland's pagan past merged with Christianity, this little coastal village nestled at the edge of the world can feel like the very place civilisation began.

There's a finality about a trip to Gleancolumbkille, a feeling of destination's end once you arrive, for it truly does feel like the end of the line; the last outpost of humanity before you're swallowed by the sea. Although I'm a native of the county, I've been to mainland Europe more times than I've been to Glencolumbkille, which is slightly ridiculous when you think about it.

Dooey Hostel

Last year, in mid September the weather gods decided to smile upon us one last time before grim bleak autumn laid claim to its dreary throne once again and I was determined to make the most of it. Like a maniac, I began hurling things into the Paddy Wagon (my car) and set a course for the remote coastal village, hell bent on imprinting my brain with some vestiges of an experience that remotely resembled a summer holiday – however brief. Since I didn't know the area I figured I'd find a hostel and spend the night having a drink or six with the locals (research), and set out walking in the morning. The distance involved also played a part in this decision, as a two hour drive tends to dull one's appetite for outdoor activities or anything remotely strenuous.

I arrived in Gleancolumbkille and pulled over to ask a man for directions to a hostel. I've stayed in a lot of hostels but the Dooey Hostel, built into the hillside, with a bird's eye view overlooking the horseshoe bay, is right up there with the best of them. On arrival a friendly man with a strong Dublin accent warmly greeted me and, within minutes, a cup of tea and biscuits were thrust into my hand. I liked him immediately. Leo, whose mother opened the hostel many years ago, showed me around and gave me a brief rundown on the village pubs. That night after a scatter of pints and idle chat, I spaltered back up the little road to the hostel beneath a canopy of blazing stars and fell into a dreamless sleep listening to the lullaby of the waves breaking on the shore.

As I was about to set off in the next morning Leo told me about two English girls who wanted to do a spot of hill walking, but they were worried

Holy Well marking the start of the Turas

Ancient Stone Cross

about missing the bus to their next destination in Donegal Town. I found the girls and told them they could come with me and I would give them a lift to Donegal Town since it was on my way home. They were delighted and for me it was nice to have company for a change. We drove across the bay towards the cliffs with the signal tower perched on top, clearly visible from the village below. A path ran up to the tower and along the cliffs but Leo told us about an interesting holy well near the beginning of the path, so we went to investigate that first.

This strange well, buried amid an enormous pile of rocks left by visiting pilgrims, was easy to find by following the signposts. Like other holy wells and holy trees along the west coast of Ireland, it's littered with hundreds of little keepsakes and odds and ends left by those who've come to pray for Divine help. Atop the well sits an ancient stone cross and next to it a white statue keeps watch. Lying amongst the rubble are two stone slabs with crosses

Signal Tower

carved into them like casket lids. The well is part of the annual Turas, or pilgrimage, and is believed to be pre-Christian in origin. It begins on midnight on the 9th June and must be completed by sunrise. The 5 km walk is usually completed barefoot.

We left the well and cut across to the main path that brought us up hill to the signal tower at Glen Head. Compared with other signal towers along the Donegal coast this one is in remarkably good shape but sadly the entrance is bricked up. It's possible, however, to haul yourself onto one of the lower windows and peek in, but it's hardly worth the effort to look at the empty shell inside. The tower is one in a chain of twelve built by the British during the 1800s to keep watch on the coast for attacks by Napoleon. The land at the tower ends both abruptly and spectacularly in equal measures. A humble sheep fence is the only thing between you and a sheer 700 ft drop down the cliffs into the sea below. We walked along the edge, making small talk with the sheep while I regaled my two new companions with tales of previous adventures in the wilderness. Suddenly Gemma spotted a lizard in the heather and I almost broke my neck trying to catch it. I'd have given my hiking boots for a picture of a lizard but it was too fast for me and disappeared into the bog. It was grey/brown in colour and around 4-5 inches long. In my hundreds of walks through the bogs and mountains I've never once seen a lizard. But it begs the question; if lizards are cold-blooded and need the sun to function, how the hell to they manage to live in Ireland? And in Donegal of all places? Answers on a postcard to…

We continued walking until we came to the spectacular outcrop of cliffs at

Sturrall and then cut back inland until we came upon a path which we simply followed back to where we started. The walk back down the path passed some stacks of turf lying ready for collection for winter storage and, when the sandy bay came into view with the village nestled snugly behind it, and Doon Point jutting out into the sea, we had to pause and stop to take it all in and admire it in the collective silence that such natural wonders of nature will often induce.

By the time we arrived back at the hostel, word had spread that there was a free taxi heading to Donegal and I managed to find room for two more German tourists and their ridiculously swollen rucksacks. It required a Herculean effort of strength just to close the boot and more than once I heard the belly of the car making contact with the potholed uneven surface of the weathered road. When we reached Donegal Town to go our separate ways, I got out to help them with their luggage. It was a beautiful sunny day in the Diamond in Donegal and as we shook hands and bade our farewells they offered me money for petrol but I declined, and instead, insisted that they use their cash to round out a perfect day by getting some drink in and having a good time in Donegal Town later that evening. They promised me they would – I hope they did.

The cliffs at Mullaghtan looking towards Sturrall

The road home...

43

Glenveagh

GLENVEAGH

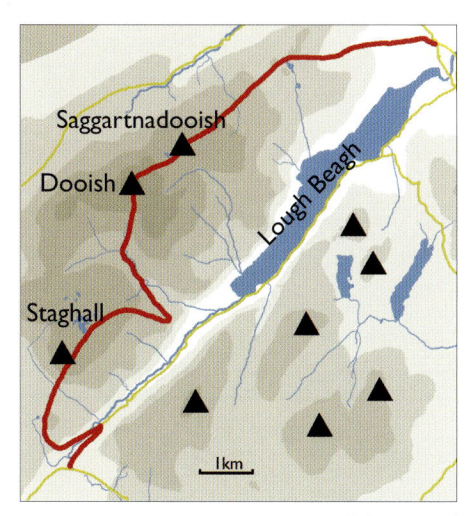

OS Map: 6
Time: 6 to 7 hours

This walk takes us through the Gleandowan side of the Derryveagh Mountains and begins at a place known as the Bridal Path which, itself, is a well known and popular walking route through the lush and magnificent glaciated valley of Glenveagh.

But as usual, for me, a clearly marked path that doesn't involve a NDE (Near Death Experience) is much too civilised and pedestrian for my feral tastes and I find that the general magnificence of Glenveagh Park can be much better appreciated from the tops of the mountains that overlook this irresistible gash in the landscape. Unlike my other walks, this one doesn't end up in a convenient loop that brings you back to the starting point. This little escapade will take you right across the mountains and spit you out at the gates of Glenveagh National Park, roughly 12 km from where you started, so you'll have to arrange a lift or be prepared to start hitching. (Bear in mind that a 12 km walk through the mountains, time-wise or physically, is in no way comparable to a 12 km walk along a footpath). The park organises walks with professional guides who have a vast knowledge of the area, but if you're deciding on bringing a group of walkers into the park yourself, please phone the park in advance to let them know how many is in your group and where you intend to go. This is especially important during September to February as this is the time for the deer cull and it's best to avoid wearing a deer suit with a pair of antlers glued on your head.

The Bridal Path begins on the road

The Bridal Path

between Churchill and Doocharry (R254) and is marked on the OS map. Head down the Bridal Path into the park and go through the gate in the deer fence, making sure to close it after you, and head down the path towards the Lough Gleann Bheatha in the distance. Across the valley to your left, on the far side of a stream, you'll see another smaller path bravely blazing a trail up the side of the mountain and disappearing over the horizon; this little path will take us where we want to be. Go up this path as far as it takes you (it doesn't go very far) and when it abruptly ends, follow the stream on your left until you reach a tiny pond-sized lough called Lough Sallagh. Avoiding the hilltops to your right and left, make for the gap of relatively level ground between the two peaks until you come to a wide sweeping glen, dissected in the middle with medical precision by a stream called the Alteann Burn.

It was on the banks of the Alteann Burn where I stopped to rest, toiling with the dilemma about the best possible route to continue travelling, peering blankly into my map and scratching my head with the seriousness of a professional code breaker; things a normal person would have figured out days ago. The thing about this walk is there's simply so much to see but it's very hard to see it all in one day without the aid of artificial respiratory equipment and a team of scantly clad NFL cheerleaders spread out along the entire route to spur you on when your life's flashing before you eyes from exhaustion. Do you stay to the high ground and take in all the views from the peaks? Or do you shimmy along the edge of the mountains, missing the views from the peaks, but availing of the stunning scenery in the Glenveagh Valley, which includes some truly breathtaking views and one very nice waterfall? It's a tough one now, it really is, so I tried to squeeze in a little of everything. The thing about staying to the peaks is that the views may be wonderful, but you've seen them all before, albeit from a different angle and perspective. There'll be all the usual suspects: Errigal, Aghal More, Aghla Beg, Muckish and the latter half of the Derryveaghs. But the view into Glenveagh from the cliff tops is both mesmorising and unique – a one off – but there's a snag here too, I'm afraid. The cliffs along the edge of the Glenveagh slope awkwardly at a fantastically inconvenient angle, making walking extremely difficult, very hard work and, basically, no damn fun at all. The ground is hazardously uneven, there's far too much grasping at handfuls of vegetation to maintain balance, reducing your progress to that of drunken stumbling wreck, and in the latter stages it involves grappling with rocks and boulders in an exhausting effort to proceed. To travel 100 yards in this wretched manner requires the equivalent amount of energy one might expel on an average marathon.

To try and take advantage of the best points on this walk, while avoiding the worst, head to the top of Staghall Mountain (486m) and across Lough Naweeloge and come back down towards the cliffs at Binnanean to gawp down into the glen for a hawk's eye view of Louch Gleann Bheatha and Glenveagh Castle.

Arguably the main attraction to Glenveagh Park, the castle's early history is one of tragedy and heartbreak which resulted in the infamous

Looking back from Staghall along the Bridal Path

Up top looking across to the far side of the glen towards Farsuallop

Glenveagh Evictions; a microcosm of what was happening all over Ireland at the time.

Between 1857 and 1859, John George Adair, a blue-blooded land speculator from Laois, bought the Glenveagh, Gartan and Derryveagh Estates after a tour of the area; a total of 28,000 acres. He began work on Glenveagh Castle in 1867.

Built by local labour, the construction of his Victorian highland retreat marked a period when high society began to view the great outdoors as fashionable, romantic and desirable, as opposed to previous generations who saw the wilderness as little more than an eyesore. To help raise capital from his newly acquired lands, he introduced black-faced mountain sheep, probably the only farm animals that could survive on the brown and purple heather-covered hills. The introduction of sheep, however, would mark the beginning of all the trouble that has come to mar this beautiful area. Despite having no fences to guard his immense estates, Adair built a pound to hold any animals that happened to stray onto his property and erected a police barracks to enforce his rule. Obviously the local tenants on his estates, who had used the land as commonage for generations, had no way of preventing their animals from straying on to his property. Fines were imposed for the return of animals that ended up in his pound and he had several men arrested and marched to Lifford Jail for alleged sheep theft, before they were found to be innocent. Strange behaviour for a man who was once a Tenant's Rights candidate (in the Limerick constituency) and claimed a desire to: *"open up the land of these remote districts and improve the conditions of the people."*

The situation deteriorated even further with the arrival of several Scottish shepherds. The shepherd's steward, James Murray, blamed locals for the loss of 85 sheep, when, in fact, it was later discovered they had died from exposure while the remainder of the lost animal skins turned up in his cottage.

Hold up! Scottish shepherds? Go back to the story of Hughie Sweeney and Lough Altan. Didn't Mr. Oban Woodhouse, who evicted Hughie from his cottage at Lough Altan, end up having to sell his botched summer home (Altan Farm) to a Scottish shepherd for £50? I'd bet my hat that one of these Scottish shepherds that arrived at Glenveagh ended up buying Altan Farm, especially when we consider the dates and the close proximity of the two locations – I'm starting to feel like Colombo or Shaggy from Scooby Do!

Anyhow, back to the story. After the Scottish shepherd, James Murray, blamed the locals for sheep rustling,

Looking down through Glenveagh

he obviously became a big hit with everyone, so much so that in a scene straight out of John B. Keane's *The Field*, his corpse was discovered on the mountainside with his head cracked opened with a rock.

Nobody seems to know who relieved Mr. Murray of his brains on the mountainside but Dan Mór Sweeney (a cousin of Hughie) was one of five Sweeneys arrested at Adair's behest after the murder. Dan had already made plans to emigrate to Australia and left soon after the incident but Adair insisted the police take out a warrant for his arrest. Dan heard the news in Liverpool and returned to Glenveagh of his own free will and surrendered himself to the warrant, but not the charge. The police failed to match Dan's footprints to those found at the scene and their case fell apart. Dan was tried and acquitted which sent Adair into complete meltdown and he recorded in writing:

"I decided to apply one of the oldest principles in English law, now enshrined in the Malicious Injuries Act, and make the people of the district responsible for the crimes committed."

The police's failure to make a conviction only strengthened his belief in a conspiracy against him and sealed the fate for over 200 souls. Figures vary on exactly how many people were evicted, but from April 8th to April 11th 1861, Adair had 47 families uprooted from their homes in Derryveagh, levelling 42 homes in the process, in a mass eviction which cleared 11,000 acres of land from human habitation, despite pleas from the clergy and concern in Parliament where his actions were debated. Eight months after the evictions, the local church made a deal with Adair to ship able-bodied young adults to Australia in an 'assisted emigration scheme,' which was preferable to starvation in the bog. In a grand and final insult, so befitting of the man, Adair had the top soil from the gardens of the evicted families dug up and transported to the castle to provide a fertile basis for his flower gardens. In Churchill, on the far side of the mountains, down a wee road with a line of grass in middle, there stands the remains of a little stone cottage with a plaque attached to the gable which quietly commemorates the ter-

Churchill Stone Cottage and plaque commemorating the Glenveagh evictions

rible injustice and suffering that took place.

Nobody knows for sure who killed James Murray but to this day the people of Glendowan assert that Dan Mor and his cousin, from Ardlaghan, were on the mountains together and that Murray fired on them with a revolver. The revolver jammed and it's said that Dan Mor, only 19, tackled the imposing figure of Murray and, in the ensuing fight, Dan's

Halfway up Dooish looking at middle of 'veaghs looking towards Poisoned Glen and Slieve Snacht

cousin hit Murray over the head with a rock for fear Murray would get the better of Dan and get the gun working again and kill them both. There's another story which asserts that Murray's killer was Dougal Rankin, Murray's wife's lover, and lodger in Murray's house. It is recorded that Rankin wore Murray's best suit of clothes to Murray's funeral. Personally, I'd like to think it was Hughie Sweeney from Lough Altan. He had a damn good motive at least. He was evicted from his home at Lough Altan only to see it taken over by a Scottish shepherd. Was the Scottish shepherd a Mr. Murray? So many questions, so few brain cells. I've already devoted far too much time to this. We have to get back to the walking, but let me just tie things up as best I can.

Adair died in 1885 whereupon the castle was passed into the care of his wife, Cornelia. After her death in 1921, the castle fell into decline and was occupied by both the Anti-Treaty and Free State Army forces during the

View from the Astelleen Waterfall

in 1984 and the castle followed two years later in 1986.

Now, where were we? Right – the cliffs at Binnanean. From here continue on until you reach the spectacular Astelleen Waterfall which spills over the cliffs like a thread of liquid silk. This inspiring flashpoint, where the Astelleen Burn surrenders itself to

The Astelleen Burn

Irish civil war. Glenveagh's next owner was Professor Arthur Kingsley Porter, of Harvard University, who came to Ireland to study archaeology and culture. He purchased the castle in 1929 but he mysteriously disappeared on a visit to Inisbofin Island. Good Lord! Henry McIhenny, an Irish/American from Philadelphia, whose father grew up in Milford, bought the castle in 1937. He set about restoring it and developing the gardens and in 1975 he agreed the sale of the estate to the Office of Public Works allowing for the creation of a national park. In 1983 he bestowed the castle to the nation. Glenveagh National Park opened to the public gravity and slides into the valley below, is one of the highlights of Glenveagh and no trip through these mountains would be complete without it. Such stunning views seem designed solely to seduce the eyes into a state of dumbfounded wonderment, as if God is showing off, flaunting His handiwork to the bedraggled hiker with a nod and a wink. The Astelleen Burn is one of those enchanting mountain streams that invites you to jump in and move through it by way of leaping from rock to rock like an excitable ostrich. It's also a handy guide to the top of the next major point of interest, Dooish Mountain (652m) – knocked into second place for king of the Veaghs by a paltry 26 metres by the Derryveagh's highest peak, Slieve Snaght (678m). Upstream, the flow passes over huge flat slabs of rock, polished smooth from eons of erosion like the weathered shells of giant granite turtles, and trickles and plunges into countless baby waterfalls and nooks and crannies whose magical

Suspicious Deer

The Astelleen Burn gorge

Top: Muckish and the coast from the slopes of Dooish

Top of Dooish looking at Errigal and Aghla More

spell leaves you frozen in your tracks – momentarily lost – gazing intently into the depths of some curious little pool for reasons you never quite fully understand, as if gold lay shimmering on the bottom. Further up, the stream cuts an impressive gorge through the rock, which also must be explored to be fully appreciated, and at the top of the gorge there's another impressive waterfall worthy of collapsing in the grass to fully enjoy its wayward splendour. As you continue to follow the stream further into the hills, the landscape changes from brown and purple into a lush green prairie of grass. It was in this immense valley of green that I came upon a sizable herd of deer that fled, unfortunately, as soon as they spotted me. There's a herd of around 300 in the park and though I did manage to creep up on two lone deer and get a half decent picture, if you're serious about getting some good pictures of these fleet-footed and shy beasts then you'll definitely need a camera with a powerful lens.

At the junction in the stream, go right and follow it towards Dooish and then make for the summit for a well earned rest. From the cairn at the top of Dooish there's an uninterrupted view in every direction of what seems like half the county: Errigal, Aghla More, Aghla Beg, Slieve Snaght and the rest of the Derryveaghs, Muckish, the Bluestacks, the Fanad

Peninsula and the mountains and hills of Inishowen in the hazy distance stretching out to sea on a long finger of land. Impressive to say the least. From here it's simply a matter of making a beeline towards the next peak of Saggartnadooish (501m) and continuing on in this direction for Misty Lough North and down into the park where, hopefully, you'll come out at a little path that takes you through the park and back to civilisation. Avoid heading down to the lakeshore, however appealing it may seem, to complete the last stage of the journey as the ground is soft and uneven and the tall sheep-free grass has an attitude and makes a special effort to sap the remaining reserves of your dwindling energy. Take my word for it. As this is such a long, but rewarding, walk, I'd strongly advise you to pack enough food for two decent meals, as well as plenty of snacks, and a minimum of four litres of water. When I last did this walk for the purpose of this book I brought my usual one miserly packet of pasta 'n' sauce rubbish, two litres of water, and an apple. On this meagre supply of rations I was very seriously considering phoning the Donegal Mountain Rescue to arrange a 'food-drop' at the top of Dooish and was forced to drinking water from streams like a deranged yeti. Hardly what you expect from an 'expert' such as myself but these things can happen, even to

Lough Veagh and Glenveagh Castle

an expert! Trust me; bring lots of grub for this one and if you're new to hill walking then I'd leave this particular journey until you're sure of your legs and comfortable with a map.

Looking across Gola with Gweedore and Errigal in the background

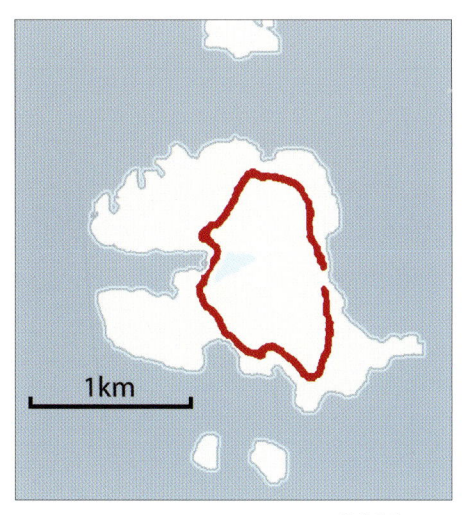

OS Map: 1
Time: Optional – just don't miss the ferry home!

GOLA

When I began this book I had no more intention of including Gola Island than I had of including Hawaii. Sure how on earth would you get there? It's been uninhabited since the mid sixties, so I assumed there'd hardly still be a ferry service for an abandoned island? Needless to say I was wrong, but I had to actually go there first to discover this little revelation.

Gola sits about a mile off the coast of Gweedore, the largest of the Gweedore islands. Its rugged windswept landscape is dictated by the wind and the sea which, even on calm days, lashes the westerly side of the island with spectacular fury. Gola has several fine beaches and secluded bays, hills and sea cliffs at the back of the island with an impressive sea arch hacked out of the rock by the unrelenting waves. Old dirt tracks and goats' paths are the main highways for getting around on this 'land that time forgot,' and the little villages and homesteads of the people who once lived there lay abandoned in a ghost town of vanishing memories, untouched and forgotten.

Exploring Gola is a simple affair and one which doesn't require a detailed map or years of hiking experience; you can walk around the entire island in a couple of hours. Be that as it may, it's still an island in the Atlantic and the sea cliffs on Gola endure a considerable battering from the ocean making them particularly dangerous. As with any place where the land meets the sea, caution must be exercised at all times.

My first trip to Gola was a camping expedition with two friends. Before we even made landfall, the scenery from the boat had our jaws dropping as we bobbed across the waves. Looking

Portacurry

back across Gweedore Bay there's a stunning panoramic view of the mainland with Errigal, as ever, looming above the entire scene like an enormous quartz pyramid-shaped watch tower.

When the little ferry/fishing boat pulled up at the tiny quay at Tra Na mBlathan we leapt off like excited dogs, dumped all our camping gear on the pier and sped off in several random directions to see what we could see. On a good day, Gola is a photographer's dream and I was hell-bent on making the most of the favourable light while it lasted. There are several marked walking paths on the island but they were duly ignored in favour of a hike up the nearest hill, Knockaculleen, for a better view. All the paths tend to only go one way as opposed to loop walks – so we invented our own loop walks. From Knockaculleen, I cut down off the hillside and on to one of the paths which led to a huge sea arch on the west of the island. At Lough Magheranagall, the only freshwater lake on the island, and within a stone's throw of the sea, I discovered a beautiful sheltered bay with a beach of round stones, sanded and polished smooth by the action of countless waves. From here I cut across the island, following a scattering of abandoned homesteads until I came to another small quay at Portacurry; a more picturesque little village you couldn't ever hope to see, and not a soul to be heard. Many of the little island homes are ruined beyond repair but I was surprised to see that many were completely intact with glass and net curtains in the windows. Some even had a coat of paint. What a strange experience it was to be the only person walking among these empty homes, this ghost town, with the lullaby of the

Old Gola schoolhouse on the shores of the Atlantic with Errigal standing watch

sea ever-present on the soft breeze. Every now and then, for the briefest of moments, you felt the surreal experience of what it might be like to suddenly travel back in time 40-odd years as you plod along in an almost respectful silence past the ghostly doorframes and windows, heavy with wonder and memories of a time lost in our collective past. Leaving Portacurry, I followed the shore back around to the pier until I came upon the old Gola schoolhouse, perhaps the only school in the entire country built, literally, on the shores of the Atlantic. You can only imagine what playtime must have been like for the kids on a hot summer's day, or how the wind must have howled outside the classroom windows during winter gales. As it turns out, Gola isn't actually completely abandoned. Although there are no shops or amenities on the island, people with a family connection to the place have returned to renovate old homesteads into summer homes and we bumped into a few people and had a friendly yarn while we were there. One such man was Eamon Breslin, who suddenly appeared at the door of an old restored barn we were staring at. Eamon told us he grew up on Gola and his mother was a teacher in the old Gola schoolhouse. I was curious to know was there ever a pub on the island, to which Eamon replied: "No, but there was no shortage of poteen!" Thoroughly exhausted from randomly exploring as much as we could before it got too dark, we went back to the little pier to gather our belongings, which were still lying there from when we'd dumped them hours ago. We pitched the tents next to a grassy spot near the pier and spent an enchanting night getting somewhat drunk and gazing across the bay at the lights on the mainland; an orange ribbon of fairy lights stretched out across the length of Gweedore, the stars overhead blazing in the sky like a rash of silver beads.

As there's no loop walks on Gola, you kind of just make things up as you go along, which is what we did. But believe me, you won't be disappointed. Admittedly, we were lucky with the weather, but it's one of the most beautiful and enchanting places I've ever seen. In the summer, the ferry to Gola leaves from Bunbeg Pier and the departure times can vary. They can, however, be located in any shop or pub in and around Bunbeg.

Morning on Gola from Pollboy

The Poisoned Glen

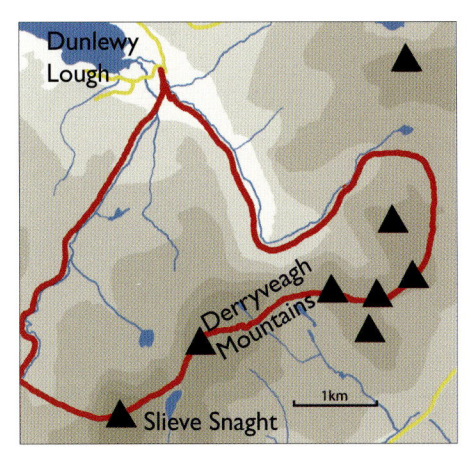

OS Map: 1
Time: 6 to 7 hours

THE POISONED GLEN

The little glacial valley that is The Poisoned Glen is one of the most instantly recognisable landscapes in Donegal. It's usually viewed from the vantage point on the main road to Gweedore which snakes around the foot of Errigal and boasts spectacular views of the valley and Dunlewy Lough. This viewpoint, however, was never quite enough for me because I wanted to see up close the place everyone was staring at. Gazing into the sweeping glen is like looking at a scene from *The Lord of the Rings*. You only have to squint your eyes to imagine hoards of screaming Orks running headlong into battle with hoards of other equally disfigured looking savages. And just like one of Tolkien's epic sagas, the region abounds with myths, legends and folklore, most of which concerns the very name of the place in question – The Poisoned Glen – but we'll get to that later.

This is definitely not a walk for beginners and will involve following the Devlin River up into the hills to the highest peak in the Derryveaghs, Slieve Snaght (678m). From here we'll traverse the undulating peaks that make up the granite spine of the Derryveaghs, walking along the cliffs for some breathtaking views down into the famous glen, through which we'll walk to round off the trip and take us back to the starting point. The Poisoned Glen itself can be found at the village of Dunlewy on the main road to Gweedore (R251). You won't need any more information than that, believe me, you'll know it when you see it.

Following the Devlin River, or any mountain stream, is a feature you'll notice with most of the walks in this book. There are several clear advantages to travelling near water and I always do so if I can. For example,

The Devlin River

ally interesting. They're always littered with waterfalls, gorges of sculpted rock and deep pools of coppery water where a man can find himself lost in a trance as he stops to rest his bones. Many of these plunge pools are deep enough to swim in and many's the hot day I found myself suddenly stripped off and swimming around in one of these little sub-zero jacuzzis. Another plus for travelling along streams is that the ground is usually harder and rocky and it's much easier to walk on than the soft wet bog. And if you're travelling solo, or camping alone, you'll never feel lonely next to a stream. The noise of the water is like a constant companion.

Anyhow, the starting point for the walk is just past the little derelict church on a little path that goes into the glen. Head up the path a little way and then cut across the Cronaniv Burn, the little stream burdened with the task of draining the glen, and head up towards the more substantial Devlin River that comes galloping down the hillside in a torrent of noise

by following a stream you dispense with the chore of having to constantly check the map to see where you are. This involves much infuriating folding and unfolding and I much prefer to study the route closely beforehand so I don't have to keep referring to the map, like the carpenter who measures twice and cuts once. I also get lost a lot – so maybe it's best to ignore that and check your map regularly. When using a stream as a guide, it becomes what's known in the business as a 'handrail feature.' It's pretty hard to get lost if you're following a stream, possible none the less, but hard. But it's more than just a matter of being practical; mountain streams are visu-

The Devlin River Gorge

and fury. After a short walk you'll come to some impressive waterfalls and some miniature white water rapids where the water is squeezed through sheer walls of rock. Further up, the river has carved out a huge deep gorge for itself out of the hill, maybe 30 or 40 feet deep in places and twice that across. Many species of tree, alien to the surrounding bog, find shelter in gorges like this and make a permanent home next to the water on the steep banks. It's like a green corridor of plant life hidden from view in the deep cleft made by the river. Descending into the gorge and walking up the Devlin River is akin to walking through a forest or a leisurely Sunday stroll through the Botanical Gardens. The canopy of greenery overheard makes it remarkably easy to forget you're in the middle of the bog. Eventually, the

The top waterfall on the Devlin River, looking back at Errigal

Cairn at the top of Slieve Snaght with Errigal, Muckish, Aghla Beg North and South, Aghla More and Mackoght in the background

Once you're on Slieve Snaght, and as you continue north east along the peaks, you're in Glenveagh National Park. At the summit there's an impressive cairn, evidence of the popularity of the highest peak in the Derryveaghs and, when you see the views, you'll understand why. From here you can see the Gweebarra River where it snakes its way into the bay and the mountains of Slieve League and South Donegal. There's also a perfect view of the smaller mountain range of Mackoght, Aghla More, Aghla Beg, Ardloughnabrackbaddy, Crocknalaragagh and Muckish, all lined up behind Errigal like the knuckles on a giant fist, known locally as The Seven Sisters. There's also the breathtaking view of almost the entire range of the Derryveaghs stretching out before you in a seemingly endless canvas of peaks and valleys and sky.

Leave the summit and go down towards Lough Slieve Snaght, which sits cradled in the valley below, and continue up the other side and across the ridge of the mountains, taking in

gorge and the trees comes to an end as the river loses its drama and once again the bog reigns supreme, but not before one last truly spectacular waterfall which comes tumbling over a tremendous staircase of rocks on a steep ridge, easily one of the many highlights of this walk.

At the top of this huge and unmistakeable waterfall, make your way to the left and up onto the hilltops at the lowest point where the rise isn't so steep, keeping Lough Agannive to your right, and head up the tiresome slope towards the rounded dome of rock that is Slieve Snaght.

all the high points along the way until you reach the very lip of The Poisoned Glen. Once you're up on the ridge traversing the peaks, the ground becomes flat and rocky making the walking easy and enjoyable. The views from up here are spectacular as you look across to Errigal, Aghla More, Muckish and Tievealehid in Gweedore. Out in the bay you can clearly see Tory Island raising out if the waves like an enormous immovable fortress in the sea.

As you approach the glen, come down off the high peaks and walk along the edge of the cliffs until you're at the very back of the glen looking up it towards Errigal. The cliffs aren't especially dangerous but take care not to walk too close to the edge as it's quite a long way down. Still, for me, the potential for danger and the calculated risks involved is all part of the allure of places like this and I'd be disgusted beyond words if someone went to the trouble of erecting a safety rail along the edge. As you make your way across, you'll encounter some deep gorges which you'll have to climb down into in order to proceed but it's easily manageable. Eventually, you should come to a gap in the rocks at the very back of the glen; the furthest point from the mouth of the glen at the village of Dunlewy, with Errigal almost directly in front of you. You'll know you're at the right spot by a huge rectangular slab of rock that dangles precariously over the edge of the cliffs

Looking into the Derryveaghs over Lough Sieve Snaght

The 'Diving Board'

Reverse view looking out of the Glen

like a diving board into the glen, not unlike a plank on a pirate ship. I don't know if this particular rock has a name, because it should have but, on the off chance that it doesn't, I hereby take this opportunity to formally christen it 'The Diving Board.' I sincerely wouldn't recommend walking to the edge of this as a sudden gust of wind would be the end of you. Just sit down and have a sandwich instead. You can be sure that there's a car of sightseers pulled over on the roadside at Dunlewy taking in the views of the glen and arguing among themselves as to whether they can see a lone figure standing on the cliffs waving back and eating a sandwich.

As I mentioned at the start of this chapter there's a legion of theories as to why this beautiful glen ended up with such an unflattering name. One explanation relates to a strain of poisonous plants that were reputed to once grow there. I even found this theory printed in a book which alluded to a wet 'spurge,' a plant that grows in the wet hollows which is poisonous to sheep. Apparently, this theory is nonsense.

Another somewhat more mythical explanation involves Balor, the ancient king of Tory Island who was notable for his evil eye, which could kill anyone it looked upon. It was prophesied that Balor would be killed by his grandson and, to avoid this, he had his beautiful daughter locked up in a tower as was customary at the time (this was long before *Sex and the City*, *Max Factor* and wireless bras) to keep her safe from perverts and peeping Toms. Word quickly spread that Balor had a beautiful daughter held captive in a tower, and attempts to breach it and liberate the fair maiden quickly became the latest craze among the locals. Eventually, Cain, father of Lugh (the Celtic God of Light and Harvest and Crafts) succeeded and carried Balor's daughter away to the mainland. Balor wasn't particularly impressed and followed them across the waves to Magheroarty where he pursued the thief across the mainland and killed him with a giant rock.

Balor and his supermodel daughter may well have passed into the annals of folklore but a rock which can still be seen lying in the entrance to The Poisoned Glen still bears his name. Legend has it that the evil one-eyed Balor was killed by his grandson, Lugh, the Celtic God of Light and the very last boulder of any significant size as you head into the glen, clearly visible from the roadside, is said to be the evil, or poisoned eye of Balor. Who knows?

The ruined church at Dunlewy

Another, less mythical, explanation which I've heard over the years concerns a row between the local landlord and his tenants. The story goes (depending on who told you and how drunk they were at the time), that the local tenants in the area had a bit of a barney with said landlord which led to some rather unsavoury behaviour on both sides. Whatever it was about, it must have been pretty serious because the outcome of this little misunderstanding led to a spate of animal poisoning and Church burning. Exactly which side burned or poisoned what, I'm not quite sure, but to this day there remains a derelict roof-less Church in the glen with suspiciously burned-looking walls.

While it's a good yarn, I've been reliably informed it's all codswallop. The derelict church is the result of the decline of the local Dunlewy Estate which meant the congregation diminished until the Church was no longer in use. Without enough people around to pay for the upkeep of the Church it simply fell into disrepair and in 1955 the roof was removed for safety reasons. The blackened walls may simply be a result of time and the rain-drenched white marble and blue quartzes which the Church is built from.

A more modern story as to why it's called The Poisoned Glen is a tad more worrying than land disputes, arson and angry giants with poisonous eyes; it's because there's … uranium in them there hills! In 1978 a Canadian company called Anglo United began a geological survey in the area to ascertain whether it was viable to begin mining for uranium. Once the news of this got out, a back to nature group based in Burtonport, called The Screamers, (called so because of their use of screaming as a form of meditation) started a campaign against the company to try and prevent them from drilling. The campaign quickly gathered momentum as more and more concerned locals joined the cause. Company vehicles were damaged and some were even burned, as well as attacks on company employees. The story regularly occupied the front page of the local papers for the next several years until it was eventually decided it was unviable to begin mining. Only one sample of commercial grade uranium was discovered by the survey in a foot core sample almost 100 feet below the rock. The survey amassed a huge amount of information about the geology of the area which could have been used by government bodies and local councils to look into the connections between cancer and natural background radiation. Unfortunately, it was such a delicate issue at the time nobody wanted to know and the information was lost or dumped.

Like all good riddles the truth is usually less dramatic than the myths that have gown around it, but I'd rather know the truth, however boring, than continue to go around spouting gibberish nonsense to whoever will listen.

After considerable research I was assured that the reason the glen got its sinister name is simply down to good old human error. The Irish word for Poison *'neimhe'* is almost the same as the Irish word for Heaven *'neamh'*. Long ago the glen was called by its original name, The Heavenly Glen, on account of its obvious beauty, but we can assume that somewhere down the line an English map maker must have made the mistake when translating the words from Irish into English. A local man told me this and that's good enough for me. I mean if you can't trust the locals…? Some food for thought as you munch on your well-earned sandwich while gazing upon the glen from your perch on the cliffs.

Continue along the cliffs until you come to a deer fence and squeeze through the wires rather than climbing over them. The staff in the park went to great trouble to erect and maintain this fence and would very much appreciate it if people didn't climb over it and damage it. Remember, you're still in the park; the fence is a deer fence and not a park boundary. Now it's just a matter of dropping off the ridges and down into the valley below, followed by a walk back to the car through the glen. The problem is that the cliffs are still too steep, so keep going until you reach a boulder-strewn area of low ground; a little dip on the ridge near Crockballaghgeeha, where there's a gentle slope that facilitates a safe walk down into the valley where you can follow the stream that runs out of Lough Beg and down into the Poisoned Glen itself.

As you make you way off the ridge and down into the valley below, you might be interested to know that you're now following an old and little known route used by the men in Gweedore on their annual trip to Scotland for the potato harvest. The Gweedore men used to walk up though Dunlewy into the Poisoned Glen, up over the mountains near Crockballagheeha and down onto the road on the Gleandowan side of the mountains at a place known as Billy's Pit (now used as a Co. Council gravel pit), near the head of Glenveagh at the start of the Bridle Path. From here they continued walking all the way to Derry to get the boat to Scotland. A feat of endurance, I think we can all agree, that really puts things into perspective when you think of some of the hardships we feel compelled to complain about on a daily basis.

Balor's Eye

Slieve League

Slieve League

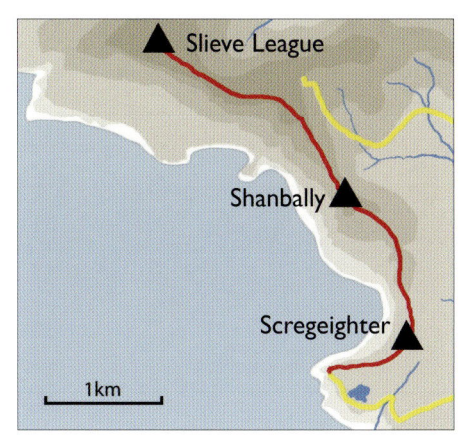

OS Map 10
Time: 3.5 hours

The epic, awe-inspiring sea cliffs at Slieve League are one of the few things I've seen in this county that can be classed as a 'wonder of the world' tourist attraction. They're Donegal's answer to the Grand Canyon or Niagara Falls, minus the agreeable weather. Now I'm not just spraying out wanton gibberish here, as I usually do. I'm basing this on the evidence I've accumulated after visiting the cliffs four times in the space of a month, because every time I was there the viewing point, where the road ends, was jammed with parked cars and people with suntans milling around, pointing cameras and looking gobsmacked. And if you waited there in the car for just a little while you were inevitably rewarded with the amusing spectacle of traumatised tourists streaming down off the hillside in Bermuda shorts and polo shirts, trying in vain to make it off the mountain before getting soaked while running headlong into a wall of freezing rain. They really should put a sign up there: BRING A COAT!

Why would somebody visit the cliffs four times in one month, I hear you ask yourself? Simple – the weather hates me. Three times I made the three hour round trip to the cliffs and three times I returned home with barely a picture taken. I even took a day off from my semi-hermit existence and made a date with the Bluestack Ramblers to help me on my quest. One fine Sunday we headed off up the cliffs with a collective spring in our step, but an hour into the walk our collective spring wasn't quite so springy anymore, as a gunmetal grey sky hurled sheets of rain-drenched wind upon us, fresh from an Atlantic squall. Wonderful, I think you'll agree. More on that particular episode later.

For years I, and many others, thought, or maybe just wanted to

Stunning views of Teelin

believe, that the cliffs at Slieve League are the highest sea cliffs in Europe but before committing to print, I figured I'd better 'research' this little fact before I went and made any rash claims about the size of our attributes. And it's a good job I checked too, because they aren't. Sadly, the title rests with the cliffs on Achill Island in Mayo. I've always suspected as much because when I lived on Achill this was a constant point of contention between myself and the locals, and very often the root cause of some considerable booze assisted debates while we argued it out into the wee small ones. Oh well, at least I can take some consolation from the little-known fact that all spot heights recorded on OS maps of Ireland are measured from the mean sea level at Malin Head. Take that Mayo! I think that just about evens things up. Where's my tablets?

Now to get to the start, go to the little town of Carrick near Teelin in South West Donegal and follow the signposts to the cliffs which are easy to locate once you've found the town. The little road climbs at an absurd angle in places, forcing you into first gear at one very steep place, and ends at a small car park with a viewing area overlooking the cliffs where they swoop down to the sea in a series of narrow ridges like dragon's toes. This is the starting point of the path that cuts along the cliffs to the farthest headland at the mountain of Slieve League itself. The path is clearly marked in the early stages and stone steps make a neat little staircase up through the bog and heather. As you progress along the path, it curves along the edge of the cliffs providing stunning seascapes of Teelin, St. John's Point and the mountains of Sligo and Leitrim. On a good day I'm told you can see all the way down the mountains of Mayo, including the holy Croagh Patrick. On most days the wind is particularly fierce and comes howling at you from the endless shimmering depths of the Atlantic, but what's more of a concern is the schizophrenic nature of the weather at this place where the land so abruptly collides with the sea. The weather on these cliffs, and all along the cliffs on the west coast, especially during the so called summer months of July and August (monsoon), is nothing short of manic. The bipolar weather changes on the cliffs in a matter of seconds but most of the time you can see the squalls of rain far out to sea as a dark curtain of moisture moving ominously towards the shore in a thick watery cloud. The plus side is that there's so much wind that these showers usually pass by pretty quickly, leaving you a little soaked but the wind will have you blow-dried again in minutes, providing you're not wearing jeans or Bermuda shorts.

Speaking of jeans, don't ever wear denim on a hill walk. It is the worst thing you could possibly wear for outdoor activities simply because when it gets wet it takes hours to dry again, by which time you'll be freezing, and when it's wet it retains no body heat whatsoever, so you may as well be naked from the legs down. Ever notice how jeans are always the last thing to

Approaching Squall

Dragon's Toes

Heading towards the One Man's Pass with the Bluestack Ramblers

Remains of the Old Chapel

overlooking the fuming sea below, or you can stay just below the ridge, where it's somewhat less exhilarating as you're sheltered from the wind, but the views just aren't as good.

Eventually you'll come to a place littered with cairns made by other hill walkers scattered all around on the rocky plateau. When you reach this little monument of scattered rocks, look for ones painted with bright yellow paint, the same gaudy yellow used for painting double yellow lines on roads. If you follow these yellow marker rocks just down over the horizon you'll come to one of the highlights of the walks, the stone ruins of a little ancient church clinging to the mountain amid a landfill of shattered rocks.

Follow the yellow rocks back up to where you were and continue along to the next major point of interest, the infamous One Man's Pass.

Tales of the dreaded One Man's Pass has always given this particular walk an added kick for me that accompanies every NDE (Near Death

dry on the clothes horse? Manmade fibres like tracksuit bottoms or proper outdoor trousers work well because they retain body heat even when they're wet and the wind dries them out again quickly.

About roughly an hour into the walk you can go by two routes to continue; you can stick to your left and clamber along the jagged ridge of the cliffs

Experience). In my wild imagination, similar to that of a sugar-crazed eight year old, I'd picture an Indiana Jones, Temple of Doom type scenario whereby I'd end up having to shimmy my way across a three inch ledge, with outstretched arms, and my back pressed up tight against a sold wall of rock behind me. Below I'd imagined a sheer drop into a frothing cauldron of sea and jagged rocks, with a few hammer head sharks and a 90 foot giant squid thrown in for good measure. Anything less than this was going to be a major disappointment.

Imagine my shock when on that first trip with the Bluestack Ramblers we first set eyes on the One Man's Pass. Unable to hide my disappointment I turned to one of the group and exclaimed, "Is that it?" You could have driven cattle across it. I'd say a three man pass would be a more appropriate title but it doesn't sound quite as catchy. The chance of a NDE are near impossible. The pass follows the knife edge ridge along the cliffs with steep sloping hills on both sides. Although the slopes are steep, you'd still be able to grab a handful of vegetation and stop yourself from falling if you did slip and, although it's a 'knife edge', sadly it's more of a butter knife than a cut throat razor.

Not long after the pass is the end of the walk atop Slieve League where the land ends and you surrender your gaze to the infinite space of the ocean.

Members of the Bluestack Ramblers brave the clouds of the One Man's Pass

On the way back through the gloom and rain of my first trip with the ramblers, I was expressing my dismay with the One Man's Pass to a lady in the group. She listened patiently while I moaned about how my expectations had been spiked with far flung tales of this terrible precipice of doom that required courage and skill to traverse and cheat death, and how

75

The real One Man's Pass from below

the pass we'd just crossed was nothing like that. It was such a bad day that we were travelling along the landward side of the cliffs to keep out of the wind, walking maybe 50–100 feet below the edge of the cliffs.

She laughed at my complaining and confided in me that she thought there was another One Man's Pass, a lesser known one along the very edge of the cliffs, and one that perhaps matched my envisioned one with the hammerhead sharks and 90 foot squids. She told me that she knew some local people in the area and they had often spoken of running up and down this One Man's Pass as a dare when they were kids. We went home and I forgot about it.

I returned about three weeks later to do the walk all over again as the weather was so bad on the first trip I didn't get many usable pictures. The sun was playing hide and seek behind a living tapestry of shifting clouds and the wind almost lifted me off my feet in places, but it wasn't raining and there were opportunities for pictures between the shifting restless light. I left the car park and began up the path and ducked under the lee side of the cliffs to keep out of the wind. On the way back I decided to walk along on the very edge of the cliffs just for the hell of it, and to my surprise I found that, there too, was a little path weaving a broken trail along the cracks and rocks along the tip of the cliffs. Eventually I came to a spot that stopped me dead in my tracks and within seconds of laying my eyes on it, I knew that I'd found the One Man's Path – the *real* One Man's Path.

Instantly, the entire walk, the three previous wasted journeys, with all their wind and rain and wasted petrol, had been paid for with one look at the exciting NDE that awaited me. And in that instant the cliffs had redeemed themselves and all was forgiven. The entire mountain is buckled and squeezed into a thin layer of bare solid rock that stretches up at a dizzying angle like a dinosaur's back. On each side there's a reasonably sheer drop to certain death, which also excludes the possibility of taking a different, easier route in order to proceed. Finally, just like it says on the tin, there's literally enough space for one person to move along, requiring a single file formation for the 40-50 feet crossing, battered by the wind all the way.

In fact, on coming down the pass I must confess to sliding along on my backside, such was the force of the wind and the immediate danger to my well being.

It took a lot for me to admit that, dammit! Indiana Jones wouldn't be caught dead sliding along on his arse.

Starring Paddy Toye as Indianna Jones

The View Down

77

The Sruell Gap

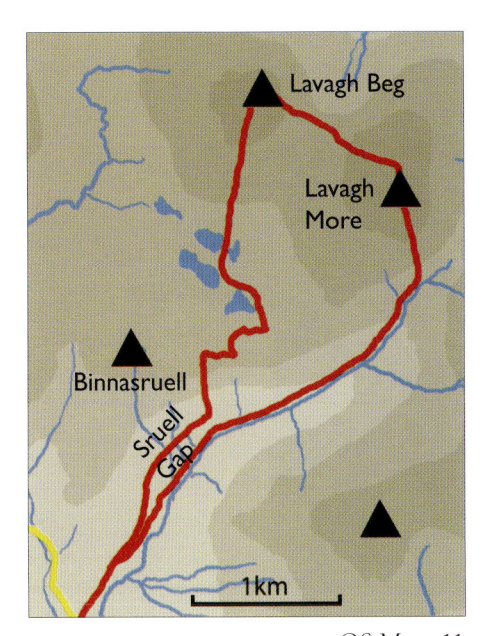

OS Map: 11
Time: 3.5 hours

The Sruell Gap

My first real attempt at exploring the Bluestacks, many years ago, involved a biker pal and two dilapidated motorbikes. Exiting the main Ballybofey to Donegal Town road, we tore down towards Lough Eske through a winding maze of lush green back roads like two maniacs from a Mad Max film who'd just been ejected from a Hell's Angels convention. The scenery we encountered around every bend, which was all new to me, contributed heavily to a continuous struggle between myself and gravity and, on more than one hair-raising occasion, I almost put the bike clean through the hedge such was the enthralling distractions of the ever changing, jaw-dropping scenery flashing by in a blur of purple, blue, green and brown. (Incidentally, despite what you may think, there's only ONE major difference between driving a car and riding a bike – you can't fall off a car.) It was only when we'd travelled right into the belly of the hills, as far from humanity as we could possibly get, that I noticed a sickening thumping in my front wheel as the air hissed out from a hole in the tyre. Fantastic, I thought, how, in the name of all that's holy, am I going to get out of this one?

Luckily Stephen knew a thing or two about bikes, which was rather fortunate as I knew absolutely nothing, and to my shocked amazement he produced a little bag of tools from somewhere and set about taking the wheel off at the side of the road while I babbled incessantly over his shoulder about rocks and mountains and streams and potential locations for our next camping trip. He carefully removed the sick wheel and gave it

79

Grey Mare's Tail on right, approach waterfall on the left

to me to hold and we took off on his bike to find a house with adequate facilities to patch the hole and re-inflate the tyre. After a short drive we spotted a lonesome farmhouse perched dramatically at the mouth of a beautiful glen with a huge waterfall tumbling down over the cliffs like a spilt glass of milk. We made a beeline for the house and knocked on the door and explained our situation to the woman who answered.

"Oh, no problem, no problem, go on out there to the shed and work away, there's tools and all out there," came the friendly reply. We thanked the kind woman and went to the shed to begin our repairs. Ten minutes later she appeared with two cups of tea and a tray of sandwiches.

"Are you hungry, boys?"

Between mouthfuls of ham and bread and gulpfuls of tea I asked the woman about the wonderful glen outside her doorstep which had me completely mesmerised, making me forget about our recent troubles with the bike. She casually answered my questions, no doubt amused at my interest at something, which to her, was probably a trivial everyday insignificance. She told me the waterfall was called The Grey Mare's Tail and, as we thanked her and left, I remember gazing at it, clutching the repaired wheel tightly in one hand, and promising myself that one day I'd return to explore it with the attention to detail befitting of such a beautiful place.

Little did I know then that when I would eventually return I'd be armed with a purpose that went slightly beyond wild curiosity. Well, that happened about six or seven years ago, and when I knew I was going to write a book about hill walking in Donegal, that beautiful glen, which we might not even have discovered if not for my puncture, was top of the list. I'm not going to even attempt to explain how to reach the starting point for this walk as the task involved would take paragraphs of confusing gibberish that would escape even my understanding. Buy an Ordnance Survey map No. 11 and scan the mountains for The Sruell Gap on the south west facing side of the Bluestacks. At the mouth of the glen follow the little path, which is marked on the map, past some old ruins of cottages, which were inhabited until recently. The path doesn't go very far and quickly disappears in the bog, but it's irrelevant anyway as we'll be breaking off to the left, straight up the hill, towards the little waterfall beside the Grey Mare's Tail. This might seem like an unnecessarily harsh way to begin a walk, slogging it up a steep hillside to the cliff tops, but I like to see what a waterfall looks like from the top as well as the bottom, and

One of the four small loughs at the top of the Grey Mare's Tail

the Grey Mare's Tail is no exception. Extreme zig-zagging is required in order to reach the top without heart failure, but you'll be surprised at how quickly you get there, and when you do you won't be complaining when you catch your first look at the glen from above.

When you near the top of the first little waterfall, where the ground starts to level out, make your way across towards the top of the Grey Mare's Tail for some high altitude watery drama as the water plunges into the valley below. From here, use the stream as a guide to its source at Lough Asgarha where your approach is greeted by a white meadow of bog cotton swaying

Coming down from Lavagh More though the gap following the Sruell River

in harmonious tune with the breeze. Among all this bog cotton sit four other little lakes nestled closely together in a hollow in the hills, which can be better viewed as you make your way up the hill towards Lavagh Beg (650m). From Lough Asgarha the summit of Lavagh Beg looks like a hop, skip and a jump, but unfortunately what you're looking at is a ridge about halfway up, and nowhere near the top, so don't get too excited – like I did. You'll get there. From these crowning peaks of the Bluestacks you can see all around on both sides of the great divide, from the Glenties side of the hills and out to the sea at Donegal Bay. From here strike out across the saddle towards the slightly taller peak of Lavagh More (671m). It was here on Lavagh More, while I was trying to shelter from the wind and rain, that I spotted a lone figure carefully adding another stone on the cairn at the top. I thought I was seeing things as the rain clouds had swept in over the mountains reducing visibility to about 50 feet of hazy shadows, so I went towards it to see if it was an apparition or a person. Clad in a heavy layer of expensive looking waterproof clothing and dark glasses, the tiny figure spoke first.

"I didn't expect to see anyone else up here today?"

"You and me both!" I replied.

"Terrible weather, maybe it might clear later?"

"Hopefully."

"Where did you come from?" she asked.

"The Sruell Gap," I answered. "And you?"

She showed me the map she was holding, wiping the raindrops from the transparent waterproof map bag. She pointed to a place at one end of the hills and, with her fingertip, traced a line to show me the route she'd taken. It was almost the whole

Bluestacks.

"Damn!" I exclaimed. "You've been everywhere!"

"Yeah."

"What time did you start walking?" I asked, expecting her to say 6am or some other unholy hour.

"11.30."

I gazed at her in a mild shock. "Hey – you don't mess around!"

"No, I don't."

I told her I was writing a book and asked her if I could take her picture. She agreed, but I could tell by the way she was watching me that she thought I was mad, or in some small way mentally unbalanced; standing there in a blizzard on the mountains in my €30 jacket that I'd bought in Penneys, grinning like a lunatic with a half eaten sandwich, frantically ransacking my rucksack to find my camera. But what she could never understand from a chance meeting on the mountainside was that what I lacked in professionalism, I would more than compensate for with sheer unbridled lunacy. In an emergency, this is usually enough to see me home. She asked me for a grid reference for the plane crash, which I gave her, and set off into the distance, disappearing into the mist like a vanishing spectre.

For myself, I was happy to drop down off Lavagh More and follow the Sruell River back through the Glen that shares its name, under the swish of the Grey Mare's Tail and back to reacquaint myself with civilisation once again.

Above: Looking up at the Grey Mare's Tail and Below: Cottage at the end of the path

Crummie's Bay

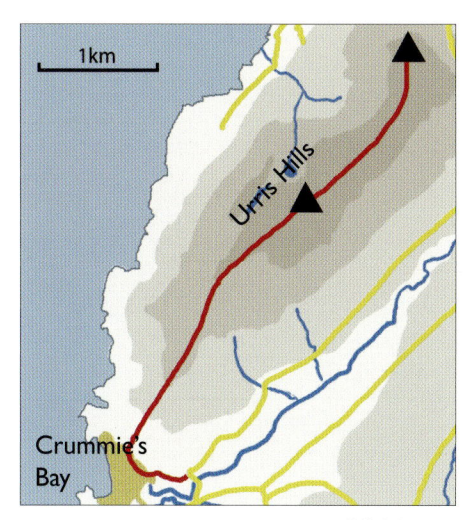

OS Map: 2
Time: 3 to 4 hours

The Urris Hills

This walk brings us to the peninsula of Inishowen, almost an island in itself. The hike begins at the little sandy beach at Crummie's Bay next to the old military installation at Dunree, Dunree Fort. The Napoleonic Fort was renovated during the late 19th century to accommodate an arsenal of heavy artillery that kept watch over the British navel fleet anchored in Lough Swilly during WWI. It's now open to the public as a war museum. On approaching Dunree, and rounding the corner, you should be able to see the bay and catch a glimpse of the beach. Pull over here and look for a little gate that leads to a sandy path which runs through the dunes and down to the beach. From the little horseshoe beach, hemmed in on both sides by brown and purple hills, there are great views across the bay to Portsalon and the golden sands of Stocker Strand. To the north, on the edge of the Fanad Peninsula, the Fanad Lighthouse can clearly be seen jutting up like a Roman candle where the land greets the sea on the horizon. Walk across the bay, crossing the Owenerk River that litters the fine sand with stones and boulders as it lazily slices through the strand into the sea, and head up onto the hills. When I did this walk it suddenly occurred to me, as I glanced back at my trail of footprints across the beach, that this is the only walk I've done that begins with getting sand on your boots. One doesn't usually associate hill walking with pristine beaches, but in Inishowen you're spoilt for choice when it comes to sand, sea and mountains. The climb towards the summit of the hills is steep to begin with but, as you near the top, it levels out somewhat into a series of gentler hills. As

Dunree Head and Crummie's Bay, with Knockalla Mountain on the Fanad Peninsula in the background

Cairn overlooking Fanad Head with Fanad Lighthouse visible at the very tip of the headland

you progress up through the ferns and heather, the views of land and sea increase in their dynamic beauty with almost every few steps, leaving you standing in breathless awe as your eyes stretch out of their sockets to take it all in.

Shortly you'll come to the first of many cairns scattered along the route. From this little pile of rocks the views are truly spectacular; to the west across the bay, the entire Fanad Peninsula spreads out before you with the Errigal/Muskish/Aghla mountain range sticking up like the battered worn teeth of an old saw while to the east lies Inishowen, a patchwork quilt of stone walls, farms and fields as far as the eye can see. At this point in the walk I came upon a path that leads all the way across the spine of the mountains. As you make your way along the path you'll catch your first peek of Lough Fad, a long narrow sliver of water squeezed between a crack in the hills. You can also see Lehan Bay and, in the distance, Dunaff Head. At the high point of 417m there's a huge cairn and a great view of Lehan Bay with its little boats tied up to the pier like brightly painted corks bobbing in the swell. The hills, I've been told, also lay claim to some scattered remains of wreckage from a plane crash. On Good Friday, 11th April 1941, a Vickers Wellington Bomber crashed into the hills killing all 6 crew. Some local men were first on the scene and helped to carry the bodies down off the hills to the village of Lenankeel where the victims were laid out in the local forge before being brought to Dunree. Down in the village the little forge still stands where a plaque was erected to commemorate the victims of the crash. I spent a good few hours searching for the remains of the wreckage but I couldn't find any, although it would probably have helped if I'd known where to look. From the high point of 417m the nature of the walk changes and is characterised by a series of steep climbs and falls as the ground dips and rises in steep troughs and peaks, with each new peak capped with a cairn. This can be a little disheartening when you first realise it but to my surprise I found it much easier going than it first appeared, which was nice. At the high point of 365m, kiss the wind, turn around and head back the way you came. On your way back, looking down towards Crunlough, the hills are scarred with what looks like the remains of old potato beds, evidence of people who once lived along the hills near the shore. The ruins of several little homes still remain and can be seen by driving down to Lenankeel and following the path along the coast, which is a nice little coastal walk in itself.

Hazy sunshine on Lough Swilly, you can just make out Mulroy Bay, Muckish and Errigal

Through the Urris Hills

Looking towards the townland of Meenderryherk

MEENDERRYHERK

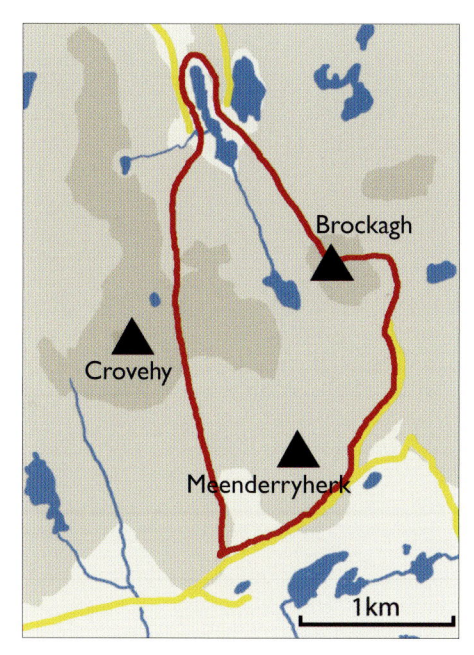

OS Map: 1
Time: 4 to 5 hours

I discovered this place by accident – a happy mistake. I randomly drove down a bog road one day (an almost weekly occurrence) and, by the time I'd realised the stupidity of my actions, I'd gone too far to turn back. Even worse, there wasn't enough space to turn the damn car around on the Stone Age little track. As I was helplessly sucked further into the laughing hills, I began to pray aloud in a feeble attempt to block out the demoralizing sounds of my car's impending destruction as it gradually began to break up like a rocket on re-entry to earth's atmosphere even though I was only doing 3 mph. However, just as I was about to start crying, lo and behold, like a lighthouse in the fog, I spotted a house in the distance. My grip on the wheel tightened with renewed determination and with teeth clenched, I sweated and cursed the last few hundred yards as if the track had been laced with landmines, almost passing out with relief when I made it onto tar again. Just your average Sunday drive.

I pulled over and stopped to have a chat with a man who was standing outside his house observing my cautious progress, no doubt wondering to himself "who in God's name is this bloody eejit coming over a road only fit for tractors and fugitives". As we talked I was mesmerised by the raw beauty of the place I'd suddenly found myself in; not spectacular or majestic by any means, but endowed with a tangible magic, a rural charm like Ireland 50 years ago, that one rarely finds these days unless you're prepared

The start of the walk

to stray from the beaten track.

We parted company and I followed the winding road past little cottages and lush emerald fields, reclaimed from the surrounding bog, until I came to a gate bearing a ramblers sign that led to a path heading off into the hills. The path looked extremely inviting and before I knew it I had the car parked and was bounding off into the hills to get properly lost this time. This little path is the beginning of a designated walking route which is marked on the OS map. It wasn't even on my list until I inadvertently stumbled upon it yet, as soon as I laid eyes on the place I knew I had to include it in this book.

To reach the starting point you can take a route which doesn't involve ruining your car, which is very handy, if not a little tricky to find. But the secretive location is part of the allure. On the road from Doocharry to Dungloe (R252) there's a little turn-off (a yellow road on the map) marked by a green letterbox at the roadside. You really have to keep your eyes peeled for the green letterbox. It's opposite Lough Sallagh, which can be seen from the road, and about 100 yards up the turn-off you'll see a little primary school on the right painted black and white. Using the map, follow this road for about a mile to the townland of Meenderryherk until you see a gate on the left at a bend in the road next to a house. The brown ramblers sign can clearly be seen on the gate at the start of the path so you'll know where you're at when you see it. Since I've discovered this little gem of a place it has become one of my favourite places to visit and, should you decide to follow me, I'll think you'll see why. My walk, which only follows the path for the first couple of miles, goes through the glen and up through a pass in the hills and down the other side into another beautiful glen wherein lies a scattering of crumbling farm houses, long since abandoned, like a little lost village in the mountains on the edge of a lake. What more could you ask for?

In the beginning the track is well defined and passes by an abandoned farmyard and several little fields and a stream on the right. It continues through this beautiful glen and up through the pass in the hills which shadow it; Crovehy (315m) on the left and Croaghavannaskea (288m) on the right (try saying that at the end of a wedding). As the path begins to rise through the hills you'll come to three abandoned stone cottages sheltered under the leafy shade of two

Ten minutes from the road

Old ruins on the track

huge sycamore trees, an oddity in itself in the bog. The little path, which is barely a goat's track in places, must have been the main access for the families who once lived there. You'll go a long way to find a nicer view from a window. As the ground rises the path gets lost but thankfully it's well signposted with marker sticks that point the way. It levels off on a rock-strewn plateau between the hills and, from here, there's a terrific view down into the next glen on the other side and The Rosses, Annagary and Bunbeg, in the distance. It's well worth taking a quick detour to one of the summits of the two hills on either side. Personally I recommend the miraculously unpronounceable Croaghavannaskea on the right, because although it's slightly smaller than its neighbour, the summit is much closer and can be reached in less than 15 minutes. From the top there's an almost perfect 360 degree panoramic view of mountains and seascape,

A view into the Rosses from the pass in the hills below Crovehy and Croaghavannaskea

Descending into the valley

with Arranmore Island basking in the bay like a giant turtle.

The plateau between the hills is where we must abandon the path and go our own way. On the map the path keeps to the high ground and snakes around the side of Crovehy but when you're standing there peering down into the next glen, with the little cottages visible in the distance, it's practically impossible to resist the urge to venture down and explore it. Only a fool or a madman would choose to ignore the enchanting sight before him; plus it's all down hill. As you descend into the valley it gently opens up before you, slowly revealing itself with each step as you instinctively make a beeline for one of the little cottages, which on closer inspection still has half of

Looking back across Lough Nagillys

its slate roof intact. At the edge of the shimmering lake (Lough Nagilly) there's another cottage which is still mostly intact but inhabited now only by sheep and swallows. The remains of other little dwellings dot the landscape as you look around, some no more than headstones peering from the ground, others just roofless walls and gables and un-glazed windows. At one time there were around nine families living in the glen but they all emigrated.

I was reliably informed by a local farmer whom I met on my walk, that the last person to live there was an 80 year old woman by the name of O'Donnell who moved out sometime in the Seventies. The story goes that a relative returned from America

Rocks which look like they've been squeezed from a tube of toothpaste at Lough Nagilly

View from Ardmeen over Lough Croangar

Rocky road to Brockagh

to take her to the States to live with them even though everyone said she was much too old to make such a trip, having spent all her life in the peaceful valley, arguing there was no way she'd acclimatise to the heat in America. It turned out she lived to be 106! The house in which she lived is the one with half a slate roof and is the first one you can clearly see as you descend into the valley. It's impossible not to think about what life must have been like living there as you wander about the heather and the ruins.

Keep going and on the right you'll clearly see another path. Follow this a little way until you come to the edge of the lake (Lough Nagilly). Go around the edge of the lake, turning back in the direction you came from, until you're walking between Lough Nagilly and Lough Nanillan, which provides an interesting view of the scenery you just passed through, not to mention some very odd shaped rocks that look like they were squeezed from a tube of toothpaste. Then make a beeline for the top of the hill on your left, Ardmeen. The twenty or thirty minute hike to the peak is arguable the hardest part of the walk so, all in all, it's not too bad. From the vantage point on the hilltop head down the other side towards Lough Crumbane until you come upon another wee track in the bog and you're on the road home again. The track, which is solid rock in places, takes you into a settlement of an abandoned farmhouse and back onto tar again in the town-land of Brockagh. From here it's a pleasant stroll back to where you started, and very easy on the eye. Both the townlands of Meenderryherk and Brockagh are absolutely stunning little gems of scenery, tucked away and hidden from the din of the modern world, like a scene from the film *The Field*. As you stroll merrily along, it's easy to imagine meeting an enraged Bull McCabe brandishing a cudgel, demanding to know the whereabouts of a certain Yank. Fortunately, all the people whom I've met were friendly, with that easy laid-back country way about them, and more than happy to pass the time of day with a bedraggled looking stranger. One elderly man even invited me into his house for 'a cup of tae and a slab of scone bread', not that I'm not saying you'll get invited in for tea, but you never know! I imagine the area is what American tourists who've never visited Ireland think of when they speak of the old country. All it's missing is a bar. If I ever win the lotto I'm going to build one out there, not to turn a profit, but just so I can take a picture of myself sitting outside it on a hot summer's day with four or five pints of stout beside me and a handful of rollups wedged behind my ear. No better way to finish a day's hiking.

Brockagh

I decided to finish the book on this walk because it sums up what's best about Donegal; although it may not have the highest mountains, and its location renders it inaccessible and remote, and in absolutely ever book ever written about Ireland it's always the last chapter, it never ceases to throw up surprise after surprise to the traveller who's willing to go that little bit further, to turn down that rocky little road on a whim and who's free enough in spirit to let their curiosity pull them over the horizon to see what might be there.

Cottage Publications

For more information and to see our other titles which include a number of books featuring Donegal, please visit our interactive website
www.cottage-publications.com
or alternatively you can contact us as follows:–

Telephone: +44 (0)28 9188 8033
Fax: +44 (0)28 9188 8063

Cottage Publications
is an imprint of
Laurel Cottage Ltd.,
15 Ballyhay Road,
Donaghadee, Co. Down,
N. Ireland, BT21 0NG